OPTIMIST
RACING

OPTIMIST RACING

A manual for sailors, parents & coaches

Steve Irish & Phil Slater

FERNHURST
BOOKS

Reprinted in 2024 by Fernhurst Books Limited

Third edition published in 2019 by Fernhurst Books Limited

The Windmill, Mill Lane, Harbury, Leamington Spa, Warwickshire. CV33 9HP, UK
Tel: +44 (0) 1926 337488 | www.fernhurstbooks.com

First edition (by Phil Slater) published in 1995 by Fernhurst Books
Second edition (by Phil Slater) published 2001 by Fernhurst Books

A catalogue record for this book is available from the British Library
ISBN 978-1-912177-18-9

The authors and publisher would like to express their considerable thanks to:
The Turkish Optimist sailors (Okyanus Arikan, Mert Aydoğan, Mustafacan Öztuncel, Kuzey Kumlali, Bulut Çanakçi), the Turkish Sailing Federation and photographer Sedat Yilmaz for the photos from Turkey © Sedat Yilmaz.
Derin Can and Dilara Soyer and their parents Anette and Orkun for the photos at Draycote Water Sailing Club by Jeremy Atkins © Fernhurst Books.
Milo Gill-Taylor for the photos at Spinnaker Sailing Club by Tim Hore © Fernhurst Books.

Front cover photograph © Mark Yuill / shutterstock.com
Back cover photograph © Sedat Yilmaz

Other photographs by:
Tom Gruitt: p9; Steve Irish: p20, 74, 87; Optimax: p71; Jeremy Atkins: p45, 62, 63, 84

Designed & illustrated by Daniel Stephen
Printed in Czech Republic by Finidr

THE AUTHORS

INSPIRATIONAL COACHES & SAILORS

Steve Irish is a world-class professional sailing coach. He has worked for the British Sailing Team, Turkish Sailing Federation and Thailand's 49er team. This has included coaching a variety of youth and junior squads, enabling 470 sailors to progress from development to Olympic-level funding – including Hannah Mills and Luke Patience – and leading 29er and 420 sailors to international success at championships such as the Youth Sailing Worlds. He coaches Optimist sailors regularly both in the UK and around the world.

He is the coach of choice among the UK national champions entering the Endeavour Trophy (the UK's Champion of Champions event) each year.

Steve's own sailing has encompassed a whole range of classes from junior and youth sailing to Olympic double-handers and high-performance skiffs. As a top Optimist sailor, Steve represented GBR internationally. He went on to become a 420 world champion and then crewed 470s, finishing 5th at the Europeans. He also sailed 49ers and Tornados internationally and subsequently competed in the twin-trapeze RS800 class, winning the national title two years running, while also claiming a podium finish at a 100+ boat RS200 nationals.

Phil Slater was a successful sailor having captained the University of London Sailing Team and won the Firefly National Championships. A doctor in Falmouth, he has been described as a 'local sailing legend' by Ben Ainslie.

Phil and his wife Jill set up a programme to encourage the local children into sailing in Optimists at Restronguet Sailing Club. Part of this group was a young Ben Ainslie, who Jill taught to sail and then rapidly progressed into the top group, run by Phil. Soon the group was one of the top Optimist fleets in the country and Phil became an RYA Optimist Racing Coach. He was the UK Optimist Team Coach at numerous championships.

He was Ben Ainslie's first sailing coach, training him to win the UK Optimist National Championships and compete in 4 Optimist World Championships. This was the start and foundation for Ben Ainslie's amazing sailing career, including winning 4 Olympic gold medals, multiple world championships and the America's Cup as tactician.

Phil still races his Firefly with Jill as well as racing a Falmouth working boat and cruising with friends around Europe.

CONTENTS

FOREWORD

I will never forget my years in the Optimist class. My family didn't have a background in sailing and so, with endless support from my parents, it was the dedicated coaches in Wales who got my sailing career started. Just as Phil and Jill Slater did for Ben Ainslie.

The competition, the camaraderie and the fun of sailing an Optimist helped develop my love of sailing and with it the results started coming, culminating in being the first girl to win the UK Optimist National Championships and the first Brit to win the Optimist Girls' World Championships. Very proud moments for any Optimist sailor!

I then moved on to double-handed sailing, first in the 420 and then the 470. I won the World Championship in both, with Steve Irish coaching me to the 420 World Championship title. At the start of my time in the 470, I was also lucky enough to be coached by Steve. He is a fantastic coach, who is patient, knowledgeable and passionate about what he does.

Good coaching is fundamental to success in the Optimist class and it is brilliant that Steve has been able to work with Phil updating the original *Optimist Racing* book, which I remember from my time in the class.

This book will show you how to sail an Optimist fast. It will teach you about techniques and tuning, boat handling and tactics – it will also offer you a lot of guidance on the physical and mental side of being a great Optimist sailor. I would highly recommend it to any Optimist sailor, no matter what level you are at in your sailing career.

Good luck in everything you want to achieve, enjoy the racing, push yourself when you are out of your comfort zone, but most importantly have fun! I hope that you really enjoy your Optimist racing and it is just the start of a really successful lifetime of sailing.

Hannah Mills, MBE
Olympic gold & silver medallist (470), World Champion (470, 420, Optimist), UK National Champion (Optimist)

INTRODUCTION

Some people look on the Optimist as a bit of a joke. It's a curvy box that kids learn to sail in! But it is numerically the biggest sailing class in the world, and ex-Optimist sailors have won many gold medals in all the dinghy classes at the Olympics. The boat is, in fact, a remarkable design – an easily-controlled thoroughbred racing dinghy that provides superb one-design racing and responds to and rewards the highest skills of top sailors.

The Optimist is sailed by more than 170,000 young people in over 110 countries. Fantastic events take place all around the world, with racing of the highest standard and great fun ashore. Each year there are open meetings, national championships, area championships and a world championship for as many as 259 sailors from 65 countries.

International Optimist racing is an adventure! It offers the chance of making lasting friendships with top sailors from other countries and representing your country in major international competitions. This book will get you into the action. Its aims are:

- To help competent Optimist sailors develop handling techniques and boatspeed. They should be able to analyse performance, coach themselves, and develop a positive psychological attitude to the stresses of competition to get to the top in national and international racing.
- To help parents analyse their own motives for supporting their children's sailing, and to avoid actions that might have a negative effect on their performance and happiness.
- To help coaches develop competitor / parent / coach relationships, to understand the constraints of children's development, and to develop race training programmes and techniques.

Performance depends on physical fitness, mental fitness, boatspeed techniques, boat handling skills, theoretical knowledge, rules knowledge, racing experience, good equipment, parental support and good coaching. Read on to find out how to achieve all these goals.

Steve Irish & Phil Slater

CHAPTER 1

Speed Basics

Sailing fast is the aim of all top sailors! It's great to leave the start line and feel the boat drawing ahead, looking back and knowing you have the speed and the other boats are not going to catch you. But how do you gain such speed?

Some people seem to sail fast naturally, while others never get a top ten result. The single thing that will help you go faster is to spend as much time as possible sailing. Get to know the feel of your boat – how she responds to changes of wind strength and wave state. You will begin to feel when the boat is balanced, when she sails herself with only small movements of the tiller. You will recognise how the balance is changed by trim, mast and daggerboard rake, sail sheeting and, upwind, the relative value of sailing fast and free or pointing higher and going a little slower.

Learn the skills of sailing upwind and down in light, medium and heavy weather, in smooth and rough water, on lakes and the open sea. Learn to sit at the boat's pivot point, leaning back, balanced, allowing your upper body to float freely as the boat moves easily through the waves. Learn efficient boat handling, power hiking and bailing. Seek to gain automatic reflex boat control. Allow – trust – your body to do the sailing while you keep your mind busy monitoring sail trim, tactics, tides, stress, etc. Learn to sail in a state of relaxed concentration, get 'in the groove', 'slip into the fast lane'…!

Speed! Feel it, live it and spot anything that might damage it.

Balance

A boat is in balance when it virtually sails itself with the rudder pointing along the centreline, producing minimal drag. A balanced boat is a fast boat; always seek balance.

- Weather helm is present when the tiller needs to be pulled to windward to keep the boat sailing in a straight line
- Lee helm is present when the tiller needs to be pushed to leeward to keep the boat sailing in a straight line
- If the rudder is needed to keep the boat on course, it is slowing you down

Too much weather helm

Too much lee helm

Balanced helm

However, a little weather helm can help upwind by generating lift and this can outweigh the added drag but be really careful it isn't too much! Aim to have the tiller so it has a slight pull and if you let go of it the boat would slowly head up. It shouldn't feel like a fight to steer. If your tiller arm is starting to ache after being on the same tack for a while you definitely have too much weather helm!

Right amount of weather helm

COR Versus COE

The Centre of Resistance (COR) is the point under the boat where the combined force of water pressure on the hull and foils (daggerboard and rudder) resisting sideslip or 'leeway' is centred. It is typically slightly behind the daggerboard.

The Centre of Effort (COE) is the point in the sail where all the sideways forces are centred.

- If the COE is aligned with the COR, the boat is balanced.
- If the COE is forward of the COR, the boat's bow will bear off from the wind. This gives 'lee helm'.
- If the COE is behind the COR, the boat's bow will turn up into the wind. This gives 'weather helm'.

Mast Rake

Rake is important in the search for a balanced boat. If the mast is raked back, the sail's COE acts behind the COR, and turns the boat into the wind. If the mast is raked forward, the sail's COE acts forward of the COR, making the boat bear away.

Daggerboard Angle

When the daggerboard is fully down you can use the elastic loop (attached to the sides of the daggerboard case) to hold it vertical, raked forward or raked aft. When the daggerboard is raked forward, the COR moves forward. When the board is raked back, the COR moves back. If the boat was in a state of balance with the daggerboard vertical, raking it forward would give you weather helm and raking it back would give you lee helm.

Centre of Effort in front of Centre of Resistance

Move helm & daggerboard back. Rake rig forward.

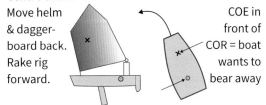

COE in front of COR = boat wants to bear away

Centre of Effort behind of Centre of Resistance

Move helm & daggerboard forward. Rake rig back.

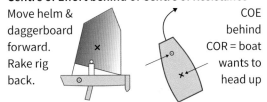

COE behind COR = boat wants to head up

Centre of Effort over Centre of Resistance

Helm in middle & daggerboard straight down.

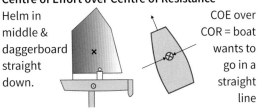

COE over COR = boat wants to go in a straight line

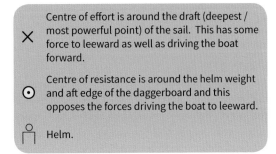

✕ Centre of effort is around the draft (deepest / most powerful point) of the sail. This has some force to leeward as well as driving the boat forward.

⊙ Centre of resistance is around the helm weight and aft edge of the daggerboard and this opposes the forces driving the boat to leeward.

⌷ Helm.

The effect of the Centre of Effort and Centre of Resistance

Daggerboard Height

In heavy weather you may need to lift the daggerboard to decrease the heeling moment and cut down weather helm. As the underwater portion of the daggerboard decreases, the COR moves up and back towards the rudder.

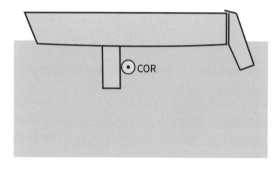

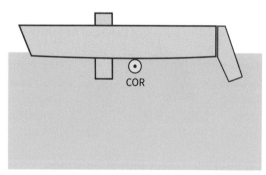

The COR moves up and back when the board is lifted

To keep the boat in balance, the mast can be raked back as the daggerboard is lifted. Lightweights will find it difficult to keep the boat flat in heavy weather, so keep balance by lifting the daggerboard with the mast upright or forward which reduces the weather helm and makes the boat easier to sail.

Sheeting The Sail

As the sail is sheeted in towards the centreline the COE moves back and makes the boat head up into the wind. This can be used to tack a stationary boat – you simply pull the sail in slowly, and the boat will spin through the wind. Similarly, balance changes when the sail is let out in gusts.

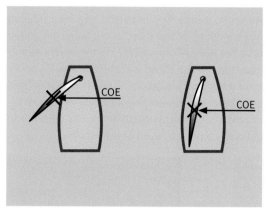

The COE moves back as the sail is pulled in

Sail Shape

Due to its cut or the way it is set, sail shape can also considerably affect the balance of a boat. An over-tight leech moves the COE back, while an open leech has the opposite effect. The sprit and kicking strap (vang) are important, because of their effects on the leech.

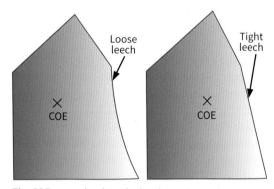

The COE moves back as the leech is tightened

Heeling (Lateral Trim)

The asymmetric underwater shape and, in particular, the effect of water pressure on the submerged lee bow, causes the boat to turn away from the immersed side. Heel can be used on all legs of the course to balance the boat and sail more quickly. For example, you can heel to windward on the beats to balance weather helm; on the run, heeling to windward balances the rotational force of the mainsail; bearing away around marks is much easier if the boat is heeled to windward.

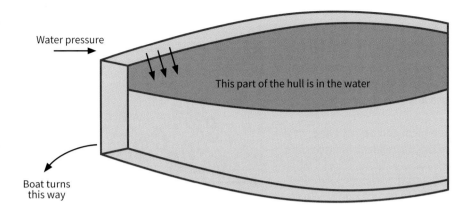

Water pressure

This part of the hull is in the water

Boat turns
this way

Allowing the boat to heel will make it want to turn

Fore-And-Aft Trim

The two aims in trimming the boat fore-and-aft are to try to prevent the bow from hitting the waves, and to try to prevent the stern dragging too deeply in the water. This is achieved with the boat sailing with its sheer line level. Lightweights will have to sit well back in moderate to fresh winds to prevent the bow from dipping.

Heavyweights have to strike a happy medium, accepting some stern drag while keeping the boat dead flat which allows the bow to lift as high as possible.

If you sit too far forward, the bow hits the waves and stops you

If you sit too far back, the transom drags due to eddies and turbulence

TOP TIPS

- Hold the tiller extension like a dagger, little finger nearest the universal joint.
- Hold the mainsheet in the same way, little finger nearest the block – thumbs up!
- Hike leaning back, knees and feet together, pulling the sheet with your elbow high.
- Keep the boat and rig balanced, and the rudder on the centreline. Try not to fight the rudder.
- Don't let the bow hit waves. Bail as soon as any water gets in the boat and sail to keep the boat dry.

PRACTICE IDEAS

Steering Without The Rudder

Using the rudder always slows the boat down. You can steer the boat without the rudder, using the following techniques:

1. A boat with lee helm can be balanced, or a balanced boat may be made to luff (turn into the wind) by:
   - Heeling to leeward
   - Bringing the COE of the sail aft – by raking the mast back, sheeting in the sail more or tightening the leech
   - Bringing the COR forward – by raking the daggerboard forward or moving yourself forward

2. A boat with weather helm can be balanced, or a balanced boat can be made to bear away (turn away from the wind) by:
   - Heeling to windward
   - Bringing the COE of the sail forward – by raking the mast forward, easing the sail or opening the leech
   - Bringing the COR aft – by raking the daggerboard aft or raising it or moving yourself towards the stern

Lash the tiller in the centre with elastic hooked around the toestraps; then practise the techniques described here.

Sailing with the tiller lashed

The sail and rig are vital components to boatspeed, so it is important that they are clearly understood.

Sail Shape

Sail shape is the key to pointing high and sailing fast.

Pointing depends on the sail's entry, which is the angle between the front of the sail and a line from luff to leech. If this angle is narrow (A) the entry is said to be flat and the boat will point high without backwinding. If wide (B), the entry is full, and the boat will point poorly.

The point of maximum depth of a sail is called the 'maximum draft'. The power or drive of a sail depends on the depth and the position of the maximum draft. Generally:
- Full sails are more powerful than flat ones
- A sail's power increases as the maximum draft moves forward
- A well-shaped sail has its maximum draft 40% to 50% of the way back from the luff (C)

In sail setting you are seeking the best compromise between pointing and power.

In smooth water the boat is not being slowed by waves and can maintain maximum speed with less power. Thus, pointing ability is most important, so set up with a flat entry, fullness further back and a flatter sail.

In rough water wave impact slows the boat and maximum power is needed to keep the speed up. Set up with the maximum draft forward, a wide entry and a full sail.

The maximum draft moves towards the relatively tighter side of the sail:

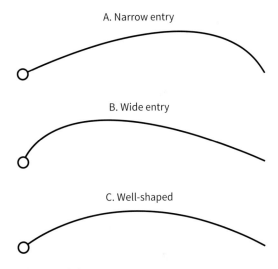

A. Narrow entry

B. Wide entry

C. Well-shaped

Different sail shapes

- Forward if the luff is tightened (e.g. if the cunningham is pulled on)
- Aft if the leech is tightened (e.g. if the kicking strap (vang) is applied or mainsheet pulled harder)
- Down if the foot is tightened (e.g. outhaul pulled in)

Sail Drive

The drive from a sail is due to the pressure difference between the windward and leeward sides. The forces trying to push the boat sideways are cancelled by the force of the water on the daggerboard and rudder foils. With a properly trimmed sail more of the forces are driving forwards.

Hooked Leech

At no time should your coach, when following straight behind your boat, be able to see the leeward side of your sail. When the leech is hooked in towards the boat's centreline, the driving force from the leech works backwards which is not good!

With a correctly trimmed sail – with the leech parallel to the boat's centreline – the boat drives forward

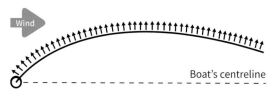

With an incorrectly trimmed sail – which hooks the leech towards the centreline – the driving force from the leech is sideways and backwards

A hooked leech is one of the most common reasons for Optimist sailors going slowly, but how does this come about?

- Excitement and over sheeting
- Not knowing what a sail looks like when it is 'just right'
- Too much sprit tension – failure to readjust the sprit for falling wind strength, so the leech tightens, and the boat stops in the lulls
- Variable wind strength – setting the sprit up for the gusts rather than the lulls
- Too much kicking strap (vang) tension – none is required upwind in an Opi, except when spilling wind
- Foot of the sail too slack
- Luff too slack or badly laced

It helps to look at the top batten. Keep this parallel to the boat's centreline when close hauled. If it angles towards the centre, the leech is hooked. Beware! Leech telltales do not always tell you the leech is hooked.

A hooked leech – one of the most common reasons for going slowly

Rig Controls

Peak

Top horizontal tie

Head

Throat

Leech

Top diagonal tie

Luff

Sail measurement bands

Sprit

Sprit tackle

Clew

Luff tie

Clew outhaul

Kicking strap / Vang

Boom strop

Mast thwart

Tack diagonal tie

Foot

Mainsheet

Bulkhead

Tack horizontal tie

Sprit

The key to understanding the sprit is to realise that the head of a sail cannot be stretched. Sprit thrust holds up the peak and tensions the leech.

Sprit on: tight leech

Sprit off: loose leech

Clew Outhaul

Besides flattening the foot, the clew outhaul moves the leech away from the mast, opening the leech and flattening the sail.

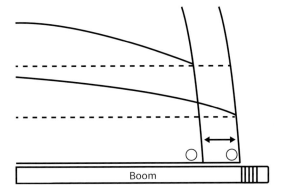

The clew outhaul flattens the sail and opens the leech

Top Horizontal Tie, Tack Horizontal Tie, Luff Ties

These alter the luff curve, which controls entry and fullness.

Top Diagonal Tie, Tack Diagonal Tie (Boom Jaw Uphaul)

These control luff length (entry and sail shape), position the sail on the mast, and control luff tension. The top diagonal tie stops the throat of the sail moving up the mast when the sprit tackle is tightened. The tack diagonal tie controls the height of the boom. It is shortened by twisting it the required number of times before hooking it onto its pin.

Kicking Strap (Vang)

This holds the boom down offwind, tensions the leech and the luff as far as the diagonal tie allows, and counters the vertical push of the sprit. If the sprit is tightened before the kicking strap, the top of the luff will form loose folds. In light weather when the luff is slack, virtually no kicking strap tension is needed. In medium weather the kicking strap should be just slack when close-hauled, but tight enough to control sail twist offwind. In heavy weather it must be tight to tension the luff and maintain leech tension when the sail is spilled.

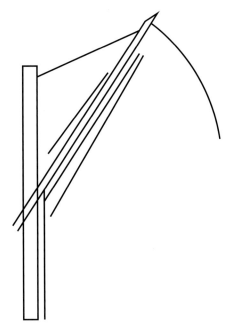

Tight sprit with no kicking strap (vang)

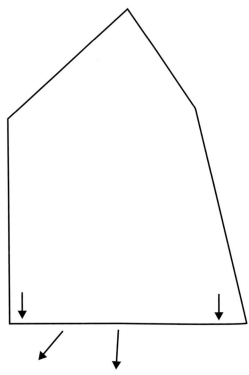

The kicking strap and mainsheet tighten the leech and the luff

Setting Up The Rig

Tie the sail ties to the boom

Thread the mast through the mast sail ties (or tie the sail ties around the mast)

Attach the top horizontal tie and the top diagonal tie (see p24)

Check the mast sail ties are the tension you want

Tie the tack horizontal tie

Attach the top of the sprit to the head of the sail

By looping the rope around the button

Attach the sprit tackle to the bottom of the sprit

Put the mast up

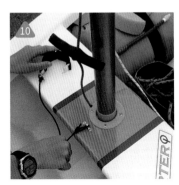

Attach the mast clamp to the mast thwart

Put the mast clamp on the mast and push it up snug to the thwart

Tighten the sprit tackle just enough to take the slack out of the top diagonal tie

Set the luff tension by choosing how many twists of the tack diagonal tie (see p24/25)

Rig the kicking strap

Apply the kicking strap (vang) tension (holding the mainsheet tight makes this easier)

Apply the desired amount of sprit tension

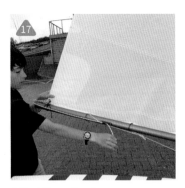

Adjust the outhaul

Finally, check the sail is still within the bands

Boom Ties

Once you have set these up you will normally leave the boom attached to the sail and roll the sail around the boom when not using it.

Mast Ties

When using a sail for the first time you will tie these to the mast, thereafter you will thread the mast through them and then adjust the tension as required for the wind strength.

Top Diagonal Tie

This tie is important to get correct. It cannot be adjusted without taking the mast down. To calibrate the rig the tie should be adjusted to keep the top of the sail at the same height. The tie should be tensioned so that, when it is in tension and the luff is slack, the sail measurement band is just below the top mast measurement band. When maximum luff tension is applied the sail measurement band will be just above the lower mast measurement band.

DID YOU KNOW?

The mark on the luff of the sail must be between the two measurement bands on the mast (see photo 18 on p23).

The gap between the sail and the mast must not be more than 10mm.

Sail Shape For Different Wind Strengths

Every time you sail record your sail shape on a Race Training Analysis sheet (see p116), along with your comments on wind and sea conditions and how the boat performed. This helps to build up confidence, judgement and boatspeed.

Light Wind Settings (Force 1-2 / 1-4 knots)

Slowly moving air will break away from a full sail, so aim to get a flat sail shape to prevent stalling and optimise acceleration / pointing. Aim for the maximum draft halfway back, with a slack luff and slack leech. You want a convex luff curve, flattening the draft and entry.

- Top horizontal tie / tack horizontal tie – set at 9mm gaps.
- Centre luff tie – no gap, but other luff ties set to give an evenly curved luff.
- Luff tension slack – put 3-4 twists in the loop of the tack diagonal tie, lifting the boom. With the luff slack the draft moves back and the entry flattens.
- Outhaul – pull out tight, which flattens sail.
- Kicking strap (vang) – totally slack so the leech is free to open.
- Sprit – slacken until a small crease appears at the throat. This shows you are not over-spritted and the leech is open.
- Boom jaws – must be tight on the mast but must allow the boom to lift as leech tension increases.

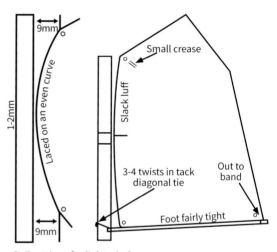

Sail settings for light wind

Gusty Winds In All Conditions

Always set up your rig, and particularly the sprit, for the lighter wind in the lulls rather than the stronger winds in the gusts. When a gust comes it will open the leech and you will be able to sail through it. A rig with correct sprit and leech tension for the gusts will have a tight hooked leech in the lulls – deadly!

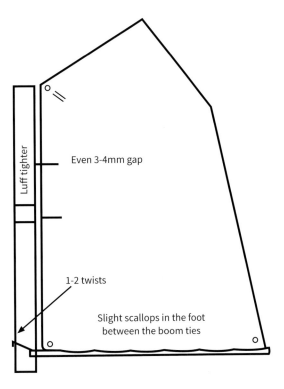

Luff tighter

Even 3-4mm gap

1-2 twists

Slight scallops in the foot
between the boom ties

Sail settings for stronger wind

Don't let the leech hook when there is a lull in the wind: adjust the sail shape for the lulls and accept that the leech will open in the gusts

Full Power Settings (Force 2-4+ / 4-11+ knots)
Set the sail with a straight luff and loose foot.

- Luff lacings, top and tack horizontal ties – adjust them to give an even 3-4mm gap along the whole luff.
- Outhaul – ease so there are slight scallops in the foot between the boom ties. If the foot is too slack the leech hooks.
- Kicking strap (vang) – just slack when the main is sheeted going upwind.
- Sprit – as for light winds with a small crease at the throat.
- Luff tension – adjust by taking off enough twists from the tack diagonal tie to firm the luff. As the wind increases the luff must be tightened.

Heavyweights
Heavy sailors can carry powered-up sails until racing is abandoned. The mast will bend, and to maintain the shape and power of the sail it is necessary to set up the top and tack horizontal ties tightly and ease the central luff ties to give an even curve with a middle lacing gap of about 9mm.

Before the mast starts to bend there is a full sail

When the mast bends, the sail becomes flatter

Depowering

You need to take another look at the rig if you're hiking hard with the daggerboard raised 10cm and raked back but you are still spilling wind in the gusts and on wave tops and are finding it difficult to keep the boat driving without heeling.

- Lace all luff ties with the eyelets with the luff of the sail just touching the mast.
- Move the leech as far away from the mast as possible by tightening the outhaul to pull the clew to the black band. This flattens the lower half of the sail.
- Ease the top horizontal tie to give an 8mm gap. This flattens the upper half of the sail. Allow for stretch – the maximum gap allowed is 10mm. Top ties must be very strong. They take all the sprit pull along the headrope as well as the sail's pull. They do most of the mast bending, and if they break the sail can tear.
- Tack horizontal tie must be tight.
- Luff must be as tight as possible. Heavyweights depower with evenly spaced luff lacings, as mast bend is flattening the entry for them.
- The kicking strap (vang) is important upwind to maintain leech tension when the wind is spilt. Apply as much tension as possible.
- Sprit must be as tight as possible, except for lightweights who, if they are really struggling, can let the sprit off so the head of the sail flaps in the gusts. Experiment with how much sprit to let off. Too much and the boat won't point, too little and it will be hard to sail flat and want to go head to wind.

To depower use a tight outhaul, tight sprit, tight luff and tight kicking strap (vang)

CHAPTER 3

Upwind Speed

The main components for good upwind speed are:
- **Boat set-up**
- **Steering**
- **Body movement**

To be the quickest upwind all of these need to be in sync and working together. Let's look at how we combine these elements to produce that blistering speed in different wind conditions and sea states.

Smooth Water

Light Wind

Imagine the water has just the smallest ripples. The wind is drifting slowly across the sail. If the sail jerks, the air flow will break away and may take as long as one minute to adhere to the sail again. During that minute you have no drive! So, the key to fast light-wind sailing is sitting absolutely still and concentrating on keeping the sail pulling by accurate steering to the slightest twitch of the telltales. Feel the wind on your cheek and look for signs of the wind on the water so that you can anticipate any changes. All your movements must be slow and smooth, whether the sheet, the tiller or your body.

Boat set-up: The sail must be set up as flat as possible so that the slow-moving air flows over it without breaking away. A full sail only has a fraction of the drive of a flat sail in drifting conditions since the air flow separates from the back half of the sail for much of the time, and total separation (stalling) occurs more easily.

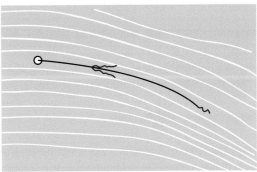

Slow air over a flat sail – all telltales (in red) are blowing back

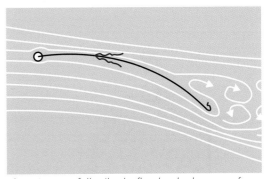

Slow air over a full sail – the flow has broken away from the back of the sail

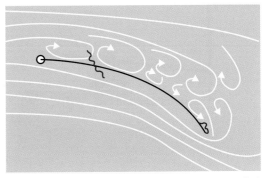

Slow air over an over-sheeted full sail – the sail is stalled with the flow totally broken away

Set up as already mentioned with mast back (to give a little rudder feel / weather helm), outhaul tight, luff slack, sail ties loose and the luff in a smooth convex curve; the leech must be slack, so set the sprit tension loose enough to get small creases at the throat.

A thin lightweight or tapered mainsheet makes sail handling easier, and sensitivity can be further increased by dropping the purchase down to a 2:1.

Steering: Keep tiller movements smooth and really concentrate on keeping the air flowing over the sail. Remember to keep the boat moving at all costs. It is tactically more important to keep in the wind patches than to sail on lifts so, if your patch is fading, head for the next one.

Body movement: It may be necessary to heel the boat to leeward, so the sail holds its shape and the

Sailing upwind in light wind on flat water

boom does not fall towards the centreline. Find a comfortable position – perhaps sitting on the bottom of the boat with your feet down to leeward keeping wind resistance down or, if the wind is a little more changeable, then squatting in the centre with your weight on the leeward foot so you can easily change your balance.

Make sure you are far enough forward to keep the transom out of the water, or eddies will form behind and slow you down. Dipping the bow does not matter if there are no waves and the boat isn't producing too big a bow wave.

Don't be negative if you are heavy. Heavy sailors have won championship races in these conditions and if you can get counting results you will be in a good position when the wind does come – in light airs the positive thinker wins!

Medium Wind

The wind is strong enough to hold the boom to leeward, you are sitting on the side and starting to use the toestraps. The key is to have the boat in perfect balance so drag is reduced and be very accurate on your telltails.

Boat set-up: The mast can now go forward to keep the boom parallel to the hull, the sail can be deepened to give more power as the air flows more easily around the sail, so ease the outhaul. Before the race, get someone to check that your leech is not hooked. If your boat is slow, the leech will almost certainly be the problem, so adjust the sprit to get the small throat crease, check the kicking strap (vang) is slack and take off a twist from the tack diagonal tie to tighten the luff a little. You will be able to sheet the sail the hardest of all in these conditions allowing you to point high in the flat water.

Steering: Concentrate on the telltails, try to keep them both flowing. If you get a small increase in breeze, see if you can just get the windward telltail to lift slightly so you can point even higher – but don't overdo it and let the boat slow. Accurate steering to the wind is critical in these conditions.

Sailing upwind in medium wind

Body movement: You are aiming to keep the boat trimmed with a slight heel to windward to keep the rudder from having weather helm. Drag from the rudder must be kept to a minimum. Sit on the side with your knees and feet together. Your feet should be ready to slip under the toestraps as the wind increases. Concentrate on your movement to keep the heel constant through the gusts and lulls, hitting the toestraps in a gust or sliding your bottom inside the gunwale in a lull. You will need to sit forward with your front leg against the bulkhead to keep the transom from dragging. When small waves start forming and splashing up the bow it's time to sit further back and sail the waves!

Heavy Weather

You are now overpowered; you need to work really hard to keep the boat flat and going fast. In stronger wind the sailor needs to take control of the boat and work hard.

Boat set-up: You now have more power being generated from the sail than you need. To lose some of that power start flattening the sail:

• Pull the outhaul tighter

• Take some twists off the tack diagonal tie to tighten the luff
• Tighten the kicking strap (vang) so that when you let the mainsheet out the boom doesn't go upwards
• Tighten the sprit so there are no creases

The loads on the main will be higher so the mast will start to bend. Adjust the mast rake so that the boom remains parallel to the boat and the overall balance remains the same. If you are struggling with weather helm in the gusts, then try lifting the daggerboard by up to 25cm. This should reduce the weather helm and the heeling moment, making the boat easier to sail.

When it gets towards survival conditions, and especially for the lighter helms, start letting the sprit off. This will look horrible but will open the leech and reduce the power dramatically. You won't point as well but at least you will be going forwards!

Steering: You are now steering to keep the boat flat, pinching to take power out of the sail. As you get a gust, hike hard and flat. If you are still

29

overpowered, then pinch slightly or, if the boat is slowing, release the sail slightly by easing the sheet by straightening your arm. As the gust goes then power the boat up by bearing away slightly and pulling the main back in. The main focus is to keep the boat flat.

Body movement: A lot of the body movement and position will be covered in the wave sailing section (p32). Remember the more you hike, the more leverage and the faster you go! Your toestraps should be set so your thighs are parallel to the boat and the gunwale is halfway along the back of your thighs. Hold the end of the tiller extension so your arm is bent, and you can still steer while sat out hard. Your mainsheet hand should be held high so you can play the sheet in the gusts without changing your grip. Keep the boat driving at speed on the beat, hiking well out in a position you can comfortably keep up for the whole race. You then have a little in reserve for short periods of extreme effort in gusts or critical moments of the race.

Have your body upright in the lulls

Extend your body in the gusts

Extending fully when required

TOP TIPS

Heavy Weather Upwind
The sail must be depowered. Set with tight luff, tight lacings, eased top tie, very tight sprit and kicking strap (vang).
- All except lightweights, keep the outhaul slack 1cm to drive through the waves.
- Sit well back to lift the bow.
- Heel 5 degrees to lift the weather bow.
- Hike hard and drive the boat. Spill wind in the gusts, don't luff.
- In lulls sheet in, lean in, bail when you can but keep moving.
- Sail free and fast. All except heavyweights will go to windward with the boom end well outside the back corner of the boat.
- Maintain boat balance by lifting the daggerboard by up to 25cm.
- Think before tacking. Look for a smoother patch, and tack on top of a wave. It can be a nightmare if you tack into a steep wave.
- Getting stuck in 'irons' during a tack is a disaster. The boat stops and then starts blowing backwards. To get out of it, point the rudder in the direction you want the stern to go, and lift the daggerboard three-quarters of the way up. When you are on a reach, begin to pull the mainsail in and sit out to get forward momentum again.
- To get home in a 'hurricane', take down the sprit and sail in on the bottom half of the mainsail.

Bailing

Keeping water out of the boat is essential to fast heavy wind sailing but it is inevitable you will ship some water in heavy winds.

Bailing is vital in heavy weather. If you can't keep your boat dry you will not survive the race! Fill a bucket with water and feel how heavy it is. Then pour it into your boat. It will spread out until it's hardly noticeable! If a few buckets of water are sloshing around they will make the boat heavy; she will not lift so well to waves; more water will break on board; and she will be harder to steer and keep upright. The weight of water to leeward counterbalances your hiking, the boat heels more, and weather helm gets extreme.

Bail early: as soon as you have any noticeable water in your boat. Don't wait until you have slowed from the weight. Remember that the more water that gets in the boat, the quicker water will come in.

Do not stop the boat to bail. If the boat is kept sailing, however slowly, when you are bailing, you will not slip to leeward:

- Ease the main enough to get the boat heeling to windward
- Move back until you have enough space to bail in front of your leg
- Keep your backside well out over the side
- Lean in and scoop forward towards the bulkhead

Use the helm to keep the boat moving smoothly ahead and a little upwind, luffing if the sail threatens to heel the boat and bearing off if the main lifts or the boat slows too much.

While keeping the boat moving, heel slightly to windward and fill up the bailer

Chuck out the water while keeping moving

Power Bailing

Now try sailing more sheeted, taking advantage of lulls in the wind or the troughs of the waves to lean in rapidly and scoop without losing any boatspeed. You will eventually find that, with tiller and main in one hand, you can luff a little while hiking, and make the water cross the boat in a little wave. You can then lean in quickly and take a scoop as the water reaches the weather side, then lean out hard while bearing off, powering the boat up and over the next wave as you dump the water.

Lean in and get a scoop in a lull   *Hike hard when you dump the water*   *And keep sailing fast*

Sailing In Waves

Basic Principles

Many styles of wave sailing can be seen at international events. Different wave conditions pose different problems, but two basic principles always apply:

- It is vital that speed is maintained and as little of the boat's dynamic energy as possible is lost negotiating each wave
- Energy loss occurs when the boat and helm are slowed by pitching, by sailing uphill and by wave impact on the bow or helm

Pitching

When a boat goes through waves, the ends of the boat move up and down. This is called pitching and this movement absorbs driving energy and slows the boat down. The more easily the ends can lift, the less energy will be lost. This can be achieved by:

- Keeping the ends of the boat as light as possible. Food, drink, sponges, painters and paddles should all be stowed by the daggerboard box.
- Sitting at the point where the boat pivots, so the boat moves without moving your body. Only the boat pitches – you maintain your equilibrium and less energy is lost. Allow your body to move with the motion of the boat, keep your core muscles relaxed and flexible. On larger waves you can help the bow rise by more forcefully rocking your shoulders back then returning to your equilibrium position.

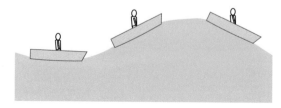

To reduce the energy lost, allow the boat to pitch

Sailing in Waves

As you go down the wave

Bear away down the wave

And lean back

So the bow rises

To the top of the wave

Go for maximum power

As you begin to go down

Bearing away

To speed up down the wave

Apart from the loss of energy and speed when pitching due to the hull moving up and down there is another effect. The rig will also rock backwards and forwards. The apparent wind moves forward as the rig rocks forward down a wave and, as the bow rises and the rig rocks back, the apparent wind moves backwards. This means that the sail is never set at the optimum angle causing loss of power and speed.

This isn't too much of a problem once you are overpowered because you can adjust to this with steering and playing the main. However, in lighter winds and big waves or chop, it can mean that, when trying to stop the boat pitching, it is better to keep the power in the sail and accept the loss from hitting the waves.

In these conditions you move your body the opposite way and, as the wave tries to lift the bow, you rock forward to try to push it down to keep the sail more stationary.

Head up as the wave lifts your bow

Power up and bear away down the wave

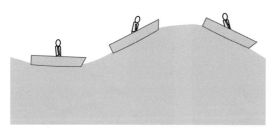

If you are trying to reduce pitching and the effect on the rig, move in the opposite way to the boat

The natural lull in the trough can also be used to heel to weather and scoop out a bailer of water

Uphill

Energy and speed are lost when the boat has to rise to go over a wave. In chop this isn't as much of a problem – pitching is more important. However, in larger waves, going up the face of the wave can slow you dramatically and cause lots of leeway.

You can steer to minimise the time going up the wave: head up as the wave lifts your bow then, on the top of the wave, bear away and power up. This is called power beating. As you get to the top of the wave and pull the power on, hike the boat level as forcefully as you can. Then move in for the short lull in the trough and as you head up the face of the next wave.

Wave Impact

The impact of waves on the bow will kill boatspeed. The weather bow is particularly important because impact here results in water coming aboard.

- Sit back to lift the bow: sailors 45kg or more sit 20cm behind the bulkhead; smaller sailors sit up to 60cm back in heavy weather
- Heel the boat 5 degrees to lift the weather bow
- Balance the boat by lifting the daggerboard
- Sail fast and free
- Allow the boat to pitch easily

Beware of burying the bow in chop – lean back to lift the bow over each wave

Wave impact on the helm can seriously stop the boat. It is important in waves to hike with your thighs parallel to the boat so your body doesn't get close to the water and you can see the waves.

Wave conditions vary massively in size, shape and angle. When sailing in waves, the key is to work out which effect is the most detrimental to boatspeed and then deploy the best technique of set-up, steering, body movement and position to counter this. And remember waves are great fun!!

Bad Habits

Take a look at top competitors at an international event sailing to windward. Most will be storming along, hiking hard and appearing to be going fast. Take a closer look. While some are sailing with a smooth continuous motion, others sail fast then pause, slowing before getting back to full speed, then slow again.

Take a look at your own sailing. Do you sail smoothly and at maximum speed, or are you a pauser? It's easy to pick up bad habits which are hard to recognise and change.

- Do you luff too much in the gusts? Is this due to letting your boat heel too much? Should you be playing the mainsheet to keep her level?
- Are you fit enough to drive fast and hard for a whole beat? Are your hiking pants comfortable?
- Are your feet supported firmly by the toestraps in the right places? Do you wriggle from one leg to the other, and what happens to the boat when you do this?
- Do you really keep the boat level or is it heeled to leeward? It's easy to get used to an angle of heel which is comfortable, but it may make the boat unbalanced. How about trying an inclinometer on your mast thwart to help change your style?
- Are you hitting waves with the bow or with your body?

When you are training or racing, try to sail the boat at 100% focus and as well as you can. Avoid picking up bad habits.

35

PRACTICE IDEAS

'Buddy' Training & Tuning

In the Optimist class top sailors have often had more than a lifetime's worth of suggestions hollered at them by well-meaning parents and coaches. It is much better to work out problems and other aspects of tuning and boatspeed for yourself, and the way to do this is by buddy training.

Find a friend who is your size and about the same speed. Get into the habit of sailing together at every opportunity. Try different aspects of tuning, technique, daggerboard or mast rake, boat trim, and styles of hiking. Check out and criticise each

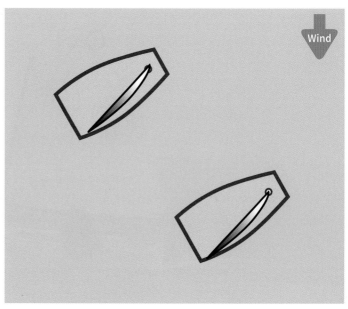

Positions for buddy training upwind

other's sailing style and sail shapes, discussing settings for the day. If one of the boats is sailing like a drain, two heads are better than one to sort out the problems. Buddy tuning gives you confidence – on the day of the big race, after sailing for five minutes with your buddy, you will know your boat is as fast as ever.

Similar techniques to buddy training can be used after the start. If you do not feel your boat is moving as she should, check a boat that is going well. What are they doing different? Check everything, then change something. Faster? Yes! Now sail away!

The standard procedure for buddy training is to sail on the same tack as your buddy, with the leeward boat slightly bow forward and the hulls two to four lengths apart. In this way, neither boat will be blanketed or backwinded by the other, and wash will not be a problem.

Sail like this until one boat draws ahead. Stop when the boat behind gets disturbed air or hits the wake. Cruise together and chat about it. Then try again, changing over the windward and leeward stations. If the same boat draws ahead, raft up and discuss why. If you can't work it out, get the slower boat sailing with the other skipper watching. If he can't spot the problem, change over with the slower helm watching the faster boat.

You can also work on boat handling with 'follow-my-leader' sessions and try close covering team-race-style duels.

Group Tuning

Used by a group (with or without a coach) to check speed, pointing, sail setting, tune and technique. After a gate start, the boats aim to get three lengths apart, close-hauled on the same tack. After a while you will see that some boats are sailing higher and some faster. Stop, compare settings, discuss, adjust and try again – to get everyone sailing high and fast!

CHAPTER 4

Downwind Speed

As with upwind speed, the main components for good downwind speed are:
*   Boat set-up
*   Steering
*   Body movement

The downwind should not be looked at as a rest before you have to go upwind again. You should not just bear away and point at the mark. Big speed and place gains can be made downwind by working the boat correctly. Let's look at some techniques you can use.

Smooth Water

Light Wind

Patience and concentration are required for long light-wind downwinds.

Boat set-up: It is important to set the kicking strap (vang) before the start for the downwind. It should be set so that, when running, it is slack enough that the leech is just opening in the gusts. You should be able to see the leech opening and closing on each gust and lull. Too little and the leech will just hang open, too much and it will remain continually closed and stalled.

As you bear away onto a run, the pressure in the sail will reduce. This will mean the sprit will be too tight. You may have to lean forward and let it off slightly to avoid a crease running from the head to the tack.

In light weather it is possible and desirable to sail downwind with the boom well forward of the mast. In this position, with the boat heeled to windward (kiting), gravity will hold the boom out. This can also help the light-weight sailor kite easier as the sail pushes the boat into windward heel.

It is common to see Optimists going downwind with too much daggerboard.

Roll your boat and take a look at how much daggerboard projects with your favourite downwind settings. On a light-wind smooth-water run the board should not project from the bottom of the boat at all.

Running in light winds with the daggerboard up

From above

From astern

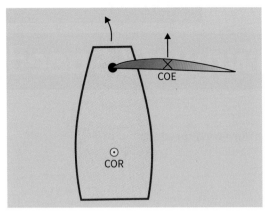
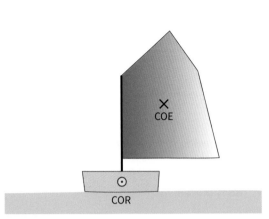

If you sail flat, the Centre of Effort (COE) of the sail is to the leeward side of the Centre of Resistance (COR) of the hull, so the boat luffs up

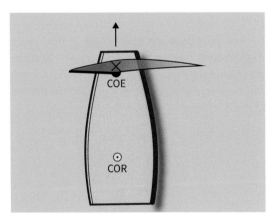
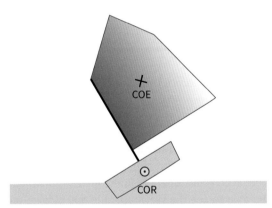

Heeling the boat to windward brings the COE more in line with the COR and the boat sails straight ahead with the rudder straight

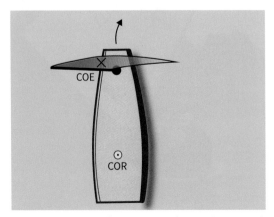
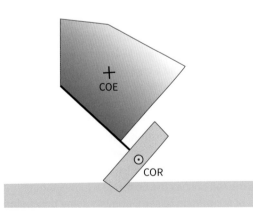

Heeling the boat too far to windward takes the COE to the windward side of the COR, so the boat bears away

Correct kiting position

Kited too far, resulting in instability and using the rudder too much

Steering: There should be no load on the rudder when on a light-wind run. The rudder should be following the boat. To achieve this the boat will have to be heeled on top of you (kited). To steer, use body weight and change the heel of the boat. More heel to windward to bear away and less heel to head up. Hold the tiller extension lightly and let the rudder follow where the boat wants to go.

Body movement: Sit well forward against the bulkhead with your front knee pointing down the gunwale. Your other leg should be tucked underneath you. You should then be able to kite without holding onto the daggerboard for support. Your front hand should be holding the mainsheet to allow trimming to help balance.

The most common mistake is to try to kite too much. This can result in wobbles and using the rudder to steer which slows the Optimist down.

Medium Wind

The boat is now starting to move nicely downwind. Most of the light wind advice still applies but with some subtle differences.

Boat set-up: The kicking strap (vang) is set up the same way as in light wind so that the leech is just opening in the gusts. The sail can be now be set at 90° to get maximum projected area since it is windy enough for the boom to stay out on its own. The sprit probably won't need letting off because there is enough wind so that the sail should keep its shape.

On the run, sit with your front knee pointing down the gunwale; do not hold the daggerboard

The daggerboard can still be raised all the way but if, as the wind increases, the boat becomes unstable then a little down will help. Still kite to reduce wetted surface area and drag.

Steering: Continue to steer with body weight and let the rudder follow the boat.

Body movement: Slide slightly further back in the boat as the wind increases to stop the nose digging in. Correct fore-and-aft trim is critical to running speed:
- If you are too far forward, the bow digs in, kicking up a wave and increasing the wash.

This can be risky for lightweights because it can lead to nose-diving and broaching.
- If you are too far back, the water begins to bubble and eddy behind the transom. This is particularly damaging when you're sailing slowly. The water should slide away without a sign that the boat has passed.

Heavyweights usually sink both the bow and stern and have to find a happy medium where drag is least. Lightweights can avoid bow and stern drag almost totally. Their problem is more one of getting back and out to keep the boat level with the bow lifting in the gusts.

Kiting

Mainsail at 90°, daggerboard up

Let the mainsail out to increase the kiting

Watch the direction of the flow of the telltales

Lean back down the waves

And as the roll increases

Trim the mainsheet in again to flatten the boat

Heavy Wind

It takes a fair breeze to get an Optimist up and planing but, once they are away, they really travel. The big danger now is a nose-dive.

Boat set-up: The kicking strap (vang) now has to be tight to keep the sail stable downwind without too much twist. Too slack and the head of the sail blows forward making a greater chance of nose-diving or the dreaded death roll.

Bring the sail in slightly from the 90° to keep the boat more stable.

The board should also not be pulled up as far to help with stability and allow more accurate and positive steering.

Steering: The boat now will not be sailed so directly downwind. The boat can be sailed slightly higher to get flow across the sail or run by the lee if it's not too unstable. Since it's windy you are likely to be encountering waves and need to steer to catch these. We will look at wave sailing in more detail later in this chapter.

Body movement: Move back in the boat as the wind increases. Ensure the bow doesn't dig in.

Once you are planing, sail the boat flat rather than kited. In semi-planing conditions, get the boat dead flat and watch out for gusts. Sail a little high in the lulls. Just as a gust is about to strike, give a pump (one per gust) and slide back in the boat in one smooth strong movement – you are away! Keep the boat level at all costs but immediately release the sheet back out so the sail is at maximum power. Trim the boat fore and aft to keep the bow just up and planing.

> ### DID YOU KNOW?
>
> Rule 42.3c allows you to pump the sail once to **initiate** surfing or planing for each gust or wave. Once you are planing you're not allowed to pump.

Downwind Wave Sailing

This is the pure essence of sailing! The pain of beating stops and magic happens. The aim is to keep sliding down the fronts or sailing the tops of the waves for as long as possible. On the front face of a wave you have clear strong wind, can slide downhill, and have the water movement with you. That's your target area. Troughs are bad news because you lose the wind and the water movement slows you down.

Catching Waves

So, you're out on a perfectly honking day with a big swell rolling in. Taking a wave is like jumping onto a moving train. You've got to run fast before you jump, so head up and sheet in as your ride approaches and pump once if you get a gust to initiate planing.

As the wave starts to lift the back of the boat, bear off hard down the wave, hike out and back, and watch out for the death roll. Feel the acceleration. The boat's got to get up to the speed of the wave or be left behind, so now lean forward to dip the nose and increase sliding. Give a hearty pump, balanced by hiking out or back, and the boat will shoot forward again, accelerating to the wave's speed and slipping down the face of the wave.

Staying On The Wave

If you shoot at full speed straight down a steep face, you will overtake the wave, reach the trough, and possibly nose-dive filling the boat with water or even pitchpole. At the very least you will slow down in the trough, having run out of wind and slope, and the wave will rush past and leave you behind. To prevent this, head up and sail along the wave or bear away and sail by the lee sailing along the wave the other way.

This takes a lot of practice to do well. This is what a lot of people call up turns and down turns.

The Down Turn
•   Heel the boat over on top of you

Catching a wave

Spot a wave you can catch

Head up to increase speed

Then bear away down the wave

And pump the main

Move your weight forward

Then back to avoid a nose-dive

Sail diagonally along the wave

Surf the wave for as long as possible

Just before you drop off the wave, head up to maintain speed for the next wave

- Sharply drop the main to 90° or maybe a bit further
- Let the rudder steer away as the heel wants to turn the boat
- Balance the boat so you ride the wave diagonally down
- Be careful not to death roll: this takes practice

The Up Turn
- Heel the boat slightly away from you so the boat wants to head up
- Sheet the main in slightly
- Let the rudder steer the boat up
- Balance the boat so you ride the wave diagonally up

Dropping Off
At some point you will fall off the wave. The answer is to realise that you are falling off the wave early and point up to keep your speed, sail high and fast along the back of the wave and in the trough, and finally bear off on the face of the next wave. In irregular waves it's necessary to watch their development like a hawk to grab a ride.

You want to be sailing down the wave

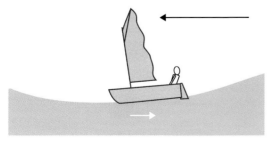

In the trough you will lose wind and the water flow is against you

Downwind sailing in waves is always different. Waves vary in size, length, angle and speed. All of these variations require slightly different styles of the above techniques. Sometimes it is easy to catch waves running by the lee, other times up turns work well due to the wave angle or sometimes just straight down the face of the wave is best when the wave is moving very fast.

Practice makes perfect! You must sail downwind in waves until your response to the characteristics of each wave becomes automatic, freeing you to ride them in the most effective manner.

Sailing By The Lee

While sailing by the lee is useful when staying on a wave, it is also a valuable skill worth working on. It gives the advantages of:
- Freedom to manoeuvre, and more options on the run
- Better chance of getting the inside position at the leeward mark
- Starboard tack advantages for the whole run
- The option to bear off, away from covering boats
- The ability to bear away to break overlaps
- Freedom to ride wave faces in either direction
- Potentially quicker than dead downwind as the wind attaches easily over the leech and the flow across the sail generates more power

Begin to practise sailing by the lee in the light winds and do not try to kite. Bear away, holding the tiller extension at the universal joint and crouching in the boat, leaning inboard. Let the sheet out progressively, keep bearing away until you are reaching along with the boom forward of the mast and the wind crossing the sail from leech to luff. You can check this by looking at the telltails. Bearing away now makes the boat actually come up into the wind and eases the sail, while heading up fills the sail with wind, heeling the boat more.

Enjoy this for a bit, then try bearing away more until the bottom of the leech starts to flick: you are near to the gybing point. Either luff a little or ease the sheet to fill the sail. Fun! To get back to a normal run again, luff up slowly and pull in the mainsheet as you do it. Well done!

When racing you would not sail so low – keep the boom at 90° to the centreline (less in strong winds). Bear away to reverse the flow on the telltails. Now try to keep the boat sailing as straight downwind as possible with the telltails still reversed.

In strong winds get your feet more into the middle, with the tiller extension on the leeward gunwale and your body leaning to leeward and facing forward. Everything works backwards! Stabilise the boat in the gusts by bearing away more and / or by pulling **in** the sheet. In the lulls power up by doing the opposite! In smooth water it's possible to kite by the lee.

Running by the lee

Reaching

Beam Reach / Close Reach

Many of the techniques used for running are applicable to reaching.

Boat set-up: Trim the sail carefully to the telltails. You are sailing the boat in the direction you want to go, so any change in wind strength or direction needs to be matched by playing your mainsheet and keeping the telltails flying.

On a reach in medium wind you often need more kicking strap (vang) than you require on a run to keep the head of the sail driving as well as

the base. The kicker is difficult to adjust but, if the reach is long, it may be worth trying to pull it on. To do this, sheet the main in hard as quickly as you can and pull the kicker tight then release the main.

Steering: Spot the mark and try to sail a straight line to it. However, if it is gusty, it may pay to come up in the lulls and bear away in the gusts to keep the best speed.

Body movement: The boat must be kept flat so there is no weather helm. Concentrate on boat trim as you would on the upwind. In the gusts try moving back to get the boat planing and remember: one pump per gust to initiate a plane.

Broad Reach

As you get broader, all the techniques become more like a run. But remember to pay particular attention to your telltails and try to keep them flying. This is where all the power comes from.

Optimist sailing on a close reach with the helm keeping the boat flat

Optimist sailing on a broad reach with the helm concentrating on the telltales

BOAT HANDLING & TACTICS

PART 2

CHAPTER 5

Basic Boat Handling

Great boat handling is a vital requirement for top level Optimist sailing. Not only does it get you around the course quicker – it also gives you confidence that you can perform in tight situations, giving you more options for overtaking.

Tacking

The Roll Tack

Boatspeed may be maintained through a tack by roll tacking. Here's how to do it:

- When you decide to tack, bear away a little and heel the boat to leeward.
- Then smoothly roll the boat right over to windward as you steer through the wind squeezing the mainsail in as you do.
- By the time the hull is pointing on the new close-hauled course, the gunwale will be touching the water and the boom should have come over your head onto the new side. Your feet should be under you, placed on the inside of the chine between the boat's bottom and side.
- Stand up, bear off a little more so that the boat is just below the new close-hauled course, ease the mainsail a little and place your back foot across the boat to the inside of the windward chine.
- Smoothly and carefully transfer your weight from one foot to the other, rolling the boat upright to her new beating trim. Squeeze the mainsail in as you do.
- Cross the boat and sit on the new windward gunwale. Do not let go of the tiller extension, but steer with your arm holding the tiller extension behind your back.
- Only when the boat is sailing well on the new tack should you change your hands around and take the tiller extension in your back hand.

When practising tacking, try counting yourself through the movements. Then try tacking as slowly as you can to the same count sequence. Next, try fast counting and tacking. Through experimenting you will find a particular rate of tacking will feel fast and comfortable.

Keep practising until you tack perfectly without needing to count or even think about what you are doing.

Don't tack on impulse. When a tack is needed keep driving, check for right-of-way boats, and look ahead for a flat patch. Tack on the top of a wave in one movement.

Timing and speed of movement change as a sailor gets bigger. Be careful to re-look at your tack as you grow. Some sailors have an awesome roll tack when they are young but, as they grow, they don't adapt the tack and it starts to look clumsy.

Sailing close-hauled

Begin to steer into the wind

Continue the turn

Roll the boat as the boom centres and squeeze the mainsail

Ease the main as the boom comes over your head and prepare to move to the other side

Bring the boat upright

Sitting on the new gunwale

Swap hands once established on the new tack and concentrate on the telltails

And get up to maximum speed on the new tack

The Max-Power Tack

Once you are overpowered going upwind you should change your style of tacking. There is no need to roll tack since you haven't the weight to pull it down as you come out the tack.

Now the priority is to come out of the tack as flat as possible. Practise crossing the boat slightly earlier and jumping straight into your hiking position. Then you can power up the boat and accelerate away.

Begin the turn

Heading into the wind

So the boom centres

Duck under the boom

And begin to cross the boat

As the sail fills move quickly to the new side

Sit down on the new side

Establishing yourself on the new tack

Before swapping hands

Double Tacking

Double tacking whilst stationary is an essential skill for Optimist sailors in the minutes before the start. While beating very slowly on starboard, tack onto port, sail for a boat length, and then tack back to starboard and stop. The entire double tack must be achieved as quickly as possible to avoid the risk of impeding a starboard tack boat. The initial tack from being stationary on starboard to port is achieved by rolling well to windward for acceleration, and then pulling the boom across to increase spin. The boat must be kept heeled right over until it points below the port close-hauled course. Then roll the boat upright, getting maximum drive from the sail.

After sailing as close as you can to the boats to windward (shouting "Hold your course!"), roll tack back onto starboard and stop the boat by holding the boom amidships for a few seconds as you step across. You are now in the enviable position of having a beautiful gap under you to power off into at the starting signal!

To create a gap

Boat 122 tacks off

Onto port

And tacks back

With a gap

To power into at the starting signal

PRACTICE IDEAS

Tacking & Double-Tacking Practice

There are lots of ways you can practise tacking.

On your own you can just go out and do lots of tacks up a short beat. This could be a mix of single and double tacks.

But with a coach, this can be made more interesting because you don't necessarily decide when to tack and there are other boats involved which makes things tighter and more competitive.

1. **Tacking on the whistle**: Start with the sailors well-spaced out on the same tack. All sailors tack when the coach blows the whistle. For variety, this exercise can be done with eyes shut!

It is easy to see who is tacking better because everyone tacks at the same time and so the sailors who make the most gains are the best at tacking!

2. **Tacking in the triangle**: Set a short start line and a short beat with a windward mark. Play it as a normal practice race but there is one additional rule – you cannot sail outside the triangle formed by the start line and windward mark. This means that, as you sail upwind, the triangle gets smaller and you have to tack more often.

It also gets tighter with other boats at the top of the triangle, really testing the boat handling.

3. **Double tacking up the line**: Set a start line and the boats all line up near the pin end. The windward boat does a double tack to create more space to leeward. As soon as they have lined up again, the next boat does a double tack, and so on until everyone is lined up at the other end of the line.

Gybing

Light Wind Gybe

Gybing can be tricky, and you must practise until it becomes automatic:

- Check that the daggerboard will not foul the boom or strop.
- Pull in approximately 50cm of mainsheet, keep the boat level or heeled a little to windward, and bear away smoothly.
- Lean in and grasp all three parts of the mainsheet about 50cm above the lower blocks but keep the tail of the mainsheet in your same hand. (This is easier than it sounds.) As the weight comes off the sheet, pull the boom across.
- Let the boat roll until the boom almost hits the water.
- Then simultaneously:
  - As the boom flies across, let go of the three parts of the mainsheet but keep the tail, ease the sheet a small amount to absorb some of the force.
  - Step across the boat and sit on the new windward side – well aft.
  - Move the tiller back to the mid-line to keep the boat sailing straight until total control is regained – you will be steering with the extension behind your back.
- Swap hands like you would in a tack.

Lower the daggerboard

Sheet in a handful of the main

Start to turn

Steer around and grab the mainsheet falls

Pull the boom over

Letting the boat roll

Move to the new side and pull the boat upright

Steer and balance the boat

Swap hands and pull the daggerboard up

Heavy Wind Gybe

In a windier gybe it can be quite scary. But don't let the boat take control of you. Be positive and definite about a windy gybe.

- Make sure you are going fast: as fast as you can before you start your gybe.
- Try to pick a good time to gybe – going down a wave, in a flat patch or in a lull.
- Don't roll the boat so much.
- The key to surviving is accurate steering of the boat. An 'S' works best, so steer up to gain speed, turn through the gybe then bear away to balance the boat.

Grab the mainsheet falls

Pull the boom over

So it crosses the centreline

Get up to the new side

To balance the boat

And get it upright and bear away to turn back

Balance the boat

Swap hands

Look for the next gust or wave to catch

Gybing Mistakes

Tripping over the daggerboard: If you turn a sharp corner at speed with the daggerboard too far down, the boat slips sideways while the daggerboard grips the water. The result is a roll to leeward as a minimum and sometimes even a capsize.

To avoid this, have the daggerboard at 30cm height. Any higher than this and it will hit the boom as it comes over. You can draw a line on the board so you know the correct position.

Broaching: Loss of control just before the boom comes over, followed by the boat screwing back onto her previous course, is due either to the boat heeling to leeward (the leeward chine digs in and steers her back up into the wind), or having the sail too far out making it harder to pull over to gybe.

Think about your timing of pulling the mainsheet over and the steering of the boat. These need to be coordinated.

Nose-diving: Nose-diving is usually caused by too much water in the boat and / or the helm not sitting far enough back. Done with style this can result in the boat rolling transom over bow, with the helm landing on the sail or even in the water ahead.

Bail regularly to ensure the minimum amount of water in the boat and sit further back.

Bear Away

A good bear away can give you a great tactical advantage for the next leg. The key is to make the turn fast and smooth and to try not to use the rudder as a brake.

- As you approach the mark, make sure that your mainsheet has no tangles in it. Hold it above your head with your mainsheet hand so it can be released easily.

To bear away, from hiking on the beat

Begin to bear away, releasing the mainsheet

Heeling the boat to windward to help the turn

As you continue to bear away

Onto the new leg

And raise the daggerboard

- As you round the mark, start the bear away by releasing the mainsheet. Lead with the mainsail, not the rudder, and don't sit in.
- The boat will heel on top of you and want to bear away. Let the rudder follow where the boat wants to go.
- Control the speed of the turn with the heel of the boat. Move in and flatten the boat to stop the turn.
- Don't forget to pull your daggerboard up and check your settings once you are going in the right direction.

Head Up

Rounding up onto the beat can be a very important part of the race. Holding a lane and keeping out of dirty air after the mark can give you a lot more tactical options.

- Push your daggerboard down early. It only slows the boat marginally and you don't want to be rushing as you need to make the rounding.
- Heel the boat to leeward to make it head up. Try to make a smooth turn coming in wide

Heading up

As you prepare to head up, lower the daggerboard

Sail to the buoy

Round up as you reach the buoy

Pull in the mainsheet to match your turn

Pulling in hand-over-hand

And hike

and leaving the mark tight so you are not in anyone's dirty air and will have an option to tack at the start of the beat.

- As you turn, pull the mainsheet in hand-over-hand matching the speed of the turn.
- Once around the mark, concentrate on the telltails and speed. Check your sail to make sure it is set right.

Other Boat Handling

Stopping

You need to be able to stop during pre-start manoeuvres, to avoid pile-ups at marks and going for the inside position, or when team racing, which can often become 'Go Slow' racing.

To slow down or stop:
- Weave about from side to side, using the rudder more than necessary
- Ease the sail or pull the sail in if running
- Sit out over the stern and sink the transom – this increases drag enormously
- Luff with the sail eased
- Push the boom out if going upwind

To stop quicker, push the boom into the wind

To stop, luff, ease the sail right out and sit over the transom to sink the stern

Accelerating

Accelerating or triggering is a vital skill to help you get away from the start line cleanly. You must have space below you at the start, having made a slow controlled approach.

Just before the starting signal, from stationary:
- Heel the boat away and head just off close-hauled with the sail just pulling.
- Roll the boat upright and head up.
- Adjust the boat's heading (with the rudder) onto the perfect close-hauled course and, at the same time, sheet in the mainsail to the beating position just over the corner of the transom, but do not over-sheet.
- Check your heel and fore-and-aft trim. Don't hit a wave!
- Apply maximum hiking power if the wind requires it and concentrate on the telltails.

Accelerating off the line

To accelerate off the start, bear away slightly

Heel the boat to leeward

Pull it upright and the mainsail in

And concentrate on the telltails

PRACTICE IDEAS

Sailing Backwards

This is worth trying now and again, for fun and as practice for getting out of irons. It is an essential skill for confident manoeuvring at the start when you often need to move back as well as forward under full control, especially if you need to re-position on the start line.

- Luff and get into irons.
- Try to steer downwind without touching the sail, going backwards on starboard tack. The stern goes in the direction the tiller points.
- Get out of irons and get sailing as quickly as possible on starboard tack.
- When getting out of irons, lifting the daggerboard will help more than pulling or pushing the sail.

If you want to go backwards faster, when head to wind, hold the boom to windward.

Push the boom out into the wind

Steer the boat in reverse

Until you can establish yourself on the new tack

Tactics is a huge subject. You should read *Tactics to Win* by Nick Craig or *Tactics Made Simple* by Jon Emmett, both also part of Fernhurst Books' *Sail to Win* series, which cover all the situations that crop up on the race course. In this chapter we'll look at the most important parts of the course.

The Start

Start priorities are:
- To get a 'front line' start.
- To have a gap to leeward for acceleration.
- To start at the right end of the line.
- Be active! Be dynamic! Be pushy! Be dominant!
- Don't hit people. Stay legal.

Starting lines in Optimist races are very congested, and a remarkable amount of boat contact, sail contact and dubious practice take place. You will survive if you keep awake with both eyes open. Shout in good time if you think somebody will foul you in any way.

Picking Where To Start

Have a good routine before the start:
- Sail upwind and feel what is a lift and what is a header. How much and how often is it shifting? Is there a reason why one side of the beat might pay? If there is, check it out by doing a split tack with your buddy.
- Decide on your strategy for the beat – go one way, tack on the shifts, try to sail to the gusts or stay with the fleet? Or a combination of these?
- Return to the start and check the line bias and get a transit if there is one.
- Make sure you check what the course board says and where the windward mark is.
- Be ready to start your stopwatch and sync it on the preparatory signal.

Now it is decision time – where to start? Match where you start to the strategy for your beat. For example:
- If you want to go right, then start to the right of the fleet so it is easier to tack.
- If it is a port-biased line and you need to go left, you might have to fight it out for the pin.
- If the wind has shifted left in the starting sequence, then you need to find a position on the line where you can tack early onto port.

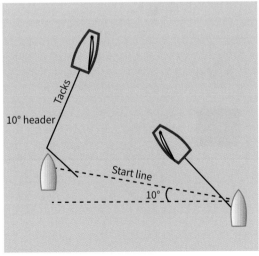

10° header

Tacks

Start line

10°

Most championship start lines have a 5-10° port-end bias: starting at port can give you an immediate advantage over the fleet; with a small header of around 10°, you can tack and cross them all!

Executing Your Start

- Learn to be confident near the line. Sail up and down it; come up to it from below; drop down onto it from above.
- Identify the rate and angle of drift of the slowest possible starboard tack approach. Use this knowledge to get to your planned starting point at the starting signal.
- Hold your position by filling your sail, gaining a little headway, then luffing until the boat stops. It will then start to slip back, so bear off, get headway again, and luff once more.
- Try to squeeze the boats to windward. This will help keep your nose ahead, so your wind is clear and you keep luffing rights. Beware getting so close to the windward boat that it touches and gets stuck alongside you. All you can do in this situation is protest, and they have ruined your start. If you push them back in anger, you're DSQ! Try to stop the windward boats sailing over you. Keep your bow ahead, point high and hold them back.
- Use double tacking (see p49) to get into gaps to windward and keep clear water beneath you. Do a 'double' at every opportunity. Starboard tacks boats will intentionally be sailing very

slowly and will not be in a position to speed up much to get you. Under RRS Rules 15 and 16 they may not alter course without giving you 'room to keep clear'. A loud hail of "Hold your course!" and / or "Room please!" may well hold them back.

- Reaching along behind the fleet on port tack with a few minutes to go, hoping to find a way through to the front-line needs practice, a good nerve, and a lot of luck! It will not work in a big fleet of top competitors.
- Make sure that you know the racing rules relating to the start perfectly; then make sure everybody around you knows that you are in control and they cannot push you around. Threaten the windward boats loudly; tell the starboard tackers to hold their course; demand 'room and time to keep clear' from leeward boats. Be noisy if necessary but keep cool!

Surviving Black Or U Flag Starts!

Think about how the fleet might react to a black or U flag. It is safer to start at an end because it is easier to tell where the line is. However, lots of sailors will think like this so the ends might get crowded. In the middle it is harder to tell where

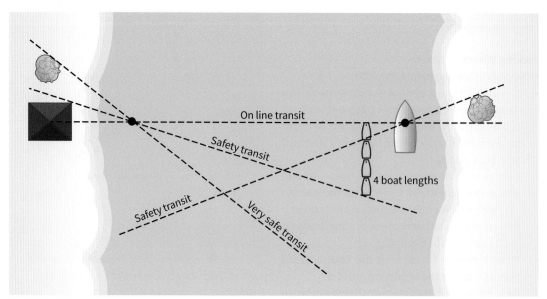

Getting transits

the line is, so sailors will be tentative. This often results in a large line sag and terrible starts out of the middle. If you can get a good transit and be confident, it is often easy to jump the fleet in the middle and have an easy, safe and good start.

Watch how the fleet lines up for the start and make your decision!

Do not keep sailing to windward if there is a general recall in a black flag start. Try not to get spotted as a premature starter by immediately stopping your boat; sit on the transom, ease the sheet and bear away.

Optimist start lines are very congested

PRACTICE IDEAS

Practising Starting

Short line exercises can be used to develop close-quarter boat handling, rule knowledge and build confidence. Depending on the number of sailors, set a reasonably short line between two marks with a mark 50m to windward for turning. Practise with sound signals at 3 minutes, 2, 1, go.

Alternative exercises are:

- Fight for the starboard end. The idea is to get into and hold the position on the line nearest to the starboard end.
- Fight for the port end. The game is to attempt to get and hold the pin end position. This is virtually impossible, but is good practice for a slow controlled approach, tacking into gaps, and double tacking.
- Place half the group on the line, and then with one minute to go the other half try to get into the front rank. To really congest the line, set up a box below the line outside which sailing is not allowed.

There are lots more variations of these exercises, so be creative and think about what you are trying to improve.

The Beat

First Half Of The Beat

If you can go straight for the first few minutes after the start and you can make your own first decision without it being forced on you by the other boats, you have made a good start.

- Don't tack too often, and never (hardly ever!) in the first 100m.
- Follow your race plan. If your start has gone wrong, look for opportunities to get clear air and then quickly get back to your race plan.
- Keep in clear air and sail fast.

Second Half Of The Beat

- Keep away from the laylines and sail the 'middle cone' unless your plan was to go fully one side for a gain.
- Think about how much risk you are taking with the fleet. If you are with the leading group, stick with them and sail fast. If you are in the pack, spot the opportunities for good shifts, gusts or clear air.
- As the mark approaches be careful to keep your air clear as the fleet compresses.

The first half of the beat will be crowded – keep in clear air

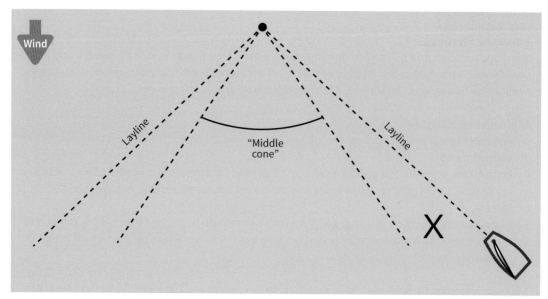

Don't sail on the layline: if lifted, you will overstand; if headed it may be difficult to tack and you might have to sail the header and lose distance

The Windward Mark

Windward Mark Approach

- Get the boat dry before arriving at the mark.
- With few boats near, you can sail fast with clear wind right up to the mark. Take your chance with a late approach. There is no need to get on the layline too early and risk a loss due to a windshift or misjudgement.
- In the 'pack' there is lots to be gained and lost. If it is very crowded, then what can often work is to come up to the starboard layline earlier. Sail right through the layline, dipping below boats where necessary until you are sure that you can lay the mark easily. Tack and sail quickly to the mark over the boats back-winding and blanketing one another to leeward.
- Never tack to leeward or in the middle of the starboard boats on the layline unless you are sure you can get around the mark. If you fail to lay the mark you may well have to gybe out.

If you try to luff for the mark and fail, you will lose many places – remember an Optimist will never luff round a mark against the tide! If you are going to hit the mark, make sure you get around it then do a 360!

Rounding The Windward Mark

- Get onto the run quickly; every two lengths sailed on a broad reach is only one and a half lengths towards the leeward mark. Do, however, give port tack beating boats room to keep clear (RRS Rule 16).
- Stay on starboard tack until you have cleared the mark area, and then sail on the most direct route to the next mark (get a transit), keeping your wind clear!
- It is often risky to gybe onto port straight away. There is less wind under all the boats on the starboard layline and a rules risk of a boat still coming upwind and having right of way. The only time this might work is when you are in last or the run is very biased to port gybe.

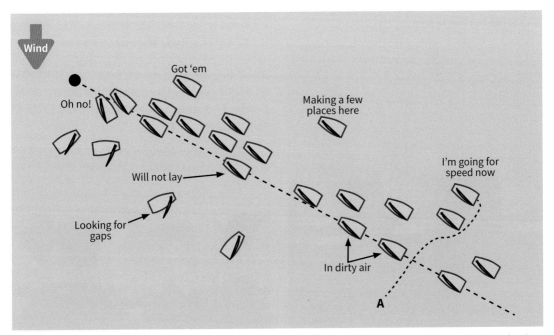

Stuck in the pack? Boat A sails through and past the starboard layline until it has clear wind. It then tacks and sails fast over the line of boats. They are all slowing one another, and some will get in trouble at the mark. Result – a few places gained.

The Reach

- If you are clear of groups, try to sail the straight-line course, using a transit if you can get one (ahead or behind).
- The first rule of reaching is 'don't get rolled'. The second rule of reaching is 'don't get rolled'! Go high if there is a bunch behind, but only high enough to keep your wind clear. Do this early and definitely: it will soon put the boats off trying to roll you.
- Often it pays to go low if there is a bunch ahead. You might get room at the next mark or even sail right under them if they get into a fight high.
- If you are heavy, ignore lightweight flyers coming up from astern. Psyche them into passing you well to windward with threats of luffing. Keep sailing the direct course. Keep low – let them go!
- Get on the inside at the mark. If you are 2ⁿᵈ or 3ʳᵈ outside, get within three lengths of the mark and then slow down hard and dip around behind the inside boat.

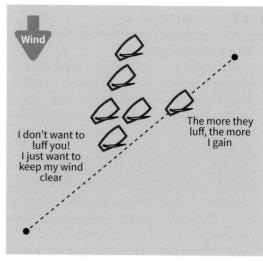

If there is no interference: sail straight for the mark

The Run

- Go for clear air, heading up or sailing by the lee to make sure you keep it
- But seek to blanket the boats that are in front of you to slow them down
- Keep an eye out for stronger wind coming down behind you and make sure you get in it

Blanketing other boats will help you catch them up, but it can be quite difficult to overtake them. Getting into stronger wind first is more likely to help you overtake them.

The reach

The run

The Leeward Mark

It is essential to start a beat from the inside position at the leeward mark. From any other position you have no immediate option of tacking clear and may have to sail for a long time in disturbed air. Like with the reach mark, if you are on the outside of a group, get within three boat lengths then slow down hard and dip round behind the inside boat. Watch out for boats ahead trying the same trick. If you were 'clear astern' of them at 'three lengths' you have no rights to room and will need to do an emergency stop.

At the leeward mark: don't get caught on the outside

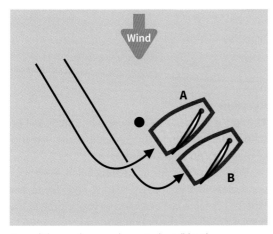

Round the mark so you leave it close (like A)

The Gate

You need to consider which mark to go around since one will almost certainly have an advantage. A good general rule is to consider the factors that might give an advantage in this order:

- Gate bias (rounding one mark involves sailing less distance)
- Can you get the inside position or would you be stuck outside a group?
- Which way do you want to go up the beat – go round the mark sending you that way
- Round the mark that puts you straight onto the lifted tack

So, if there is noticeable bias, then take it; but if you can't tell there is any bias, then look for the mark that will give you an inside rounding. If you could round either mark clean, then go for the one that takes you to the favoured side of the beat or puts you straight onto the lifted tack.

The Finish

Finish To Windward

It is easy to lose places at the finish. You must wrench your gaze from the opposition and force

The leeward mark

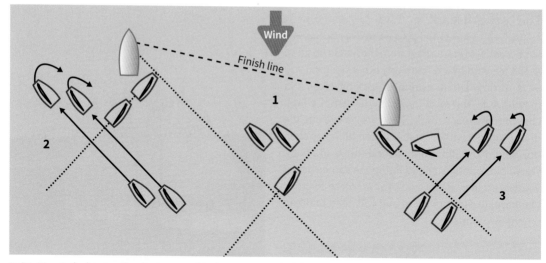

In Position 1, the boat sailing fast on port for the nearest end of the line may overtake the starboard tack pair who will sail further before finishing. In positions 2 and 3, the inner boat is blocking the outer boat from tacking for the line until the inner boat can tack and stay clear ahead.

yourself to look at the line.

If you specialise in focussed finishing you will nearly always make places. As you approach the line, ask yourself 'Which end is most downwind?' and then plan to approach that end at speed, preferably on starboard tack. On the approach, be careful you are not being blocked outside the layline and prevented from tacking.

If the port end is nearest, tack onto the comfortable dead cert layline and sail for the pin, shouting loudly to put off anybody who may be thinking of trying to squeeze in between you and the mark.

If the starboard end is nearest, get over to the starboard layline fairly soon, unless there is a large finishing boat which is taking the wind close to it.

Avoid being sailed up to the unfavoured port end of the line by boats to windward preventing you from tacking.

When defending, try to sail an opponent out past the layline for the preferred end so you can control your approach to the finishing line.

When sailing an opponent past the port end of the line, make sure you go far enough past the mark to prevent him getting an overlap when you both tack for the mark.

Reaching Finish

The race isn't over until it's over. A lot can be lost on a final reach to the finish. Remember the first rule of reaching 'don't get rolled'.

When approaching a reaching finish, keep your wind clear and go for the nearest end. Try to see whether the line has been laid as you approach the leeward mark on the previous round.

- If the windward end is nearest, go for the windward end, luffing if necessary
- If the line is square go for the windward end, but if hassled by lightweight flyers, drop down and let them luff while you go for the leeward end with speed
- If the leeward end is nearest, then try to get to it but beware of slowing and being rolled

Running Finish

To finish on a run, keep your wind clear, sail as straight as possible using a transit, and go for the nearest end. Try to sail your fastest angle as much as possible and not change your style to get to the finish – gybe if you have to.

Sometimes you can use running by the lee on starboard to great advantage so you have right of way in a close finish.

EQUIPMENT & TUNING

PART 3

CHAPTER 7

Mast Rake

Mast rake is the most mysterious element of rig control which has probably been blamed for more poor results than any of the other intangibles that go into making a successful race. What really matters is firstly that it is important in balancing the boat, and secondly that the skipper believes his rake is right.

Measuring Mast Rake

Mast rake is measured from the mast head to the top of the boat's transom using the following method:
- Make sure the mast is at the back of the deck slot, and that the step is as far forward as it can move.
- As most masts are now hollow-topped, hook the tape over the rim at the top of the mast.
- Extend the tape over the centre of the transom.
- Take the reading, where the tape touches the transom. Readings are in the range 274-290cm (108-114in). The mast step should be calibrated with marks to show the mast rake so you can adjust the rake afloat.

Setting Mast Rake

The theory of balance and mast rake was discussed in Chapter 1: Speed Basics (see p12).

You can set the mast rake by feel:
- Too much weather helm, then put the mast further forward
- The rudder feels too light then bring the mast back

The problem is that you can also change the feel by how you sit, how much heel you are sailing with, the angle of your daggerboard and how you have your sail set and sheeted.

It is identifying which of these factors needs to be changed to allow you to sail the boat perfectly in the groove that is important.

A good starting point is to keep the COE of the sail consistent and then work with the other variables to develop the correct feel. The easiest way to do this is to set the boom so it is horizontal when you are sailing upwind. This can be done on the water and checked by the sailor and coach. This means that, as the wind increases, the mast is moved forward to counter the increased sheet tension and mast bend.

The calibration of the mast foot can be recorded so that an idea can be got as to what mast rake is required for different wind strengths. This means that a good guess can be made by the sailor on the shore before they get on the water and check it.

When it goes very light, it often pays to bring the COE further back so that the rudder has some feel and gives you more feedback. This helps in the very light winds so that you can tell when the boat is driving well. In these conditions you can set up with the boom end pointing very slightly down.

Some good starting numbers for the mast rake:

Wind	cm	in
Light	274-279	108-110
Medium	279-284	110-112
Heavy	284-289	112-114

CHAPTER 8

Fast Gear

The aim is to have the perfect combination of hull, sail, spars, toestraps and controls to suit the sailor. The competitor must make his boat as individual and comfortable as his favourite trainers – but first, get a copy of the class rules and read them carefully. You will then know what you can and cannot do.

You need to be comfortable in your boat to get the maximum out of it

Make sure your hull is smooth with sharp edges

Hull

Buy a new or well cared for Optimist one-design which is at the minimum weight.

Keep it smooth and clean with sharp edges to the transom and the aft third of the chine. Smooth with 600 grade wet and dry paper, finishing with 1200 grade or polishing paste. Regularly clean and degrease with washing up liquid. Scratches and bangs can be repaired with gelcoat filler.

Always use a well-padded trolley and never let the hull touch anything else. When turning your boat over, use two people: one at each end. Turn the boat in one swinging movement through at least 90°, putting it down on the gunwale if you cannot turn through 180° in one movement.

After use, rinse the hull with freshwater, clean and dry it, and cover the bottom with a soft and preferably padded cover.

Daggerboard

Suitable foils are of vital importance to get optimum performance. Like the hull, foils must be close to the minimum weight and should be kept perfectly smooth and clean.

The daggerboard controls leeway and acts as the pivot through which your hiking balances the force from the sails. If the board is 'soft' (flexible) it will bend, and you will lose 'feel' and drive. However, there is an advantage in having a board that bends just a little in heavy weather in the biggest gusts and waves, to act as a shock absorber helping the sailor keep the boat flat and under control. Light helms need a daggerboard that is more flexible, bending under the lighter loadings they can exert. Heavier helms need progressively stiffer daggerboards, and sailors over 55kg need a totally rigid board.

The daggerboard and its box should match. The daggerboard construction and tolerances are now very small since the rules were tightened in 2005. To match the board, the daggerboard case should be packed to as narrow as possible, the minimum being 14mm. The packing must be uniform and within 30mm of the top and bottom of the case. This ensures:

- The daggerboard will not wobble from side to side in the box, making steering jerky and affecting your 'feel'
- As little water as possible is trapped in the box – water in the box adds to the boat's mass
- Minimal turbulence occurs where the daggerboard and hull meet

The rules allow stops to be fitted in the ends of the top and bottom openings of the case. These prevent the edges of the foil from being damaged, and also allow you to alter the rake of the board.

The aft bottom stop should be of maximum length (30mm) with a V cut into it to take the foil's edge. Other stops should be no bigger than 5mm. High density rubber glued in place with Sikaflex is very satisfactory.

Stops fore and aft of the daggerboard case

The daggerboard's rake can be controlled with a loop of elastic cord fixed to the sides of the case by two eyelets. This allows the board to be raked forward, back, or held vertical in the box to improve balance.

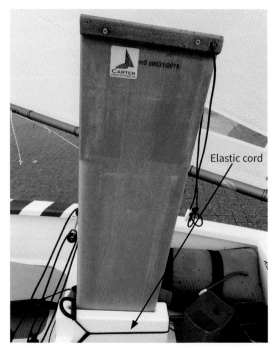

Elastic cord

The elastic cord allows you to control the rake of the board

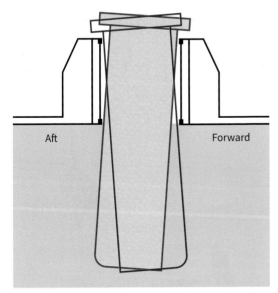

The daggerboard can be raked slightly forward or aft

Aft   Forward

TOP TIP

Beware! Hot sun can warp foils. Keep them out of the sun or, if possible, in padded bags.

Use a padded bag to protect your foils

Rudder

The rudder has a lot of work to do:
- It transmits the feel of the water and signals the state of balance of the boat to the helmsman
- It is the means of controlling the boat

To perform these functions, it is essential that both rudder blade and head are as stiff as possible so there is little or no twist between tiller and blade.

In the original class rules, the rudder blade rules were very loose. The rudder only had to fit in a rectangle. This meant that all sort of rudder rakes and designs were tried.

In 1995 these rules started to be tightened up. Since 2005 the rule has become very precise, allowing very little tolerance or change of materials. This makes it a lot easier to buy a good rudder. Be careful if you have an old boat since your rudder might not measure for racing under the current rules. An old-style rudder will also feel very different and alter your boat handling. So, even if you are a relatively new racer, it is worth getting a current-style rudder as soon as you can.

Tiller & Tiller Extension

For the tiller, a length of 600-650mm seems about right: too long and it gets in the way, too short and the steering gets heavy.

The tiller extension should be as long as possible to a combined maximum of 1200mm. Do keep an eye on the universal joint for wear and tear. It can fail quickly – which is a disaster!

Mast

For speed and high pointing, all sailors need as stiff a mast as possible. The mast thwart sleeve must hold the mast snugly athwartships, allowing maximum legal fore-and-aft movements (3mm). The mast step must have a very snugly fitting track to prevent any side-to-side movement, but the step adjuster must allow the step to slide back and forward over the maximum permitted range (3mm).

The sprit tackle must be strong, with low friction blocks, a good handle and the cleat positioned where it can be adjusted easily. There are two commonly used cleat positions:

The sprit tackle being adjusted on the water

TOP TIP

Change the sprit rope regularly else it will harden and wear at the cleating point.

- The first position, and probably the most common, is below the lower sail tie and has to be adjusted by a bouncing technique from a standing position, pushing downwards on the handle with all your body weight. Using a long low-stretch rope from the mast block to the lower block at gooseneck level minimises windage and turbulence over the sail luff. Light and inexperienced helms may struggle with this system but it can be good for the stronger heavier sailors.

The common sprit tackle arrangement and cleat position just below the lower sail tie

- The other cleat position is some 40cm below the mast block. This allows the helm to lean forward, sitting on the buoyancy bag / tank / side deck, and pull down on the handle. All sailors find this system easy to use. There is some windage penalty but, in most cases, this is more than made up for by better sail setting.

The sprit tackle is a common site of gear failure, which inevitably results in retirement. Carry a spare top block and a length of low stretch rope for rapid repairs.

The typical sprit tackle arrangement

Top Ties

These must be very strong as they take the enormous thrust of the sprit transmitted down the headrope. If they stretch, your leech tension varies, and the throat may move further from the mast than allowed by the rules (more than 10mm).

The Optimax and Optipart systems involve plugs which go in the top of the mast which the horizontal and diagonal ties attach to. The plugs also have holes which sit inside the mast to hold the wind indicator or burgee in place.

These systems are efficient but some find them difficult to adjust. Use Dyneema or Spectra of 3mm diameter and check ties for each major event and heavy weather races and replace if necessary. Watch for wear where the cringle rubs and where the ties go into the mast.

A simpler system using rope through the holes and around the mast

Whatever system is used, the key is for it to be adjustable and non-stretch.

Boom

Boom stiffness is essential to keep the sail flat in heavy weather and control the leech. A bendy boom will slacken the leech in gusts but will result in the sail becoming slightly fuller. Mast, sprit bend and sail cut allow the leech to fall off adequately in gusts for most sailors, complementing the use of sprit and kicking strap (vang).

Lighter sailors should consider using a boom which bends more to make the rig have greater automatic gust response and hence make the boat easier to sail.

All modern booms have special end fittings allowing minimum-friction double-purchase outhauls to be rigged. The rope must be low stretch. The outhaul cleat should be fitted in the middle of the boom where it can be reached easily on most points of sailing.

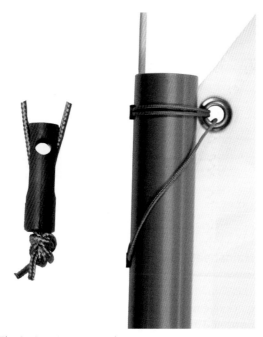

The Optimax top pins and tying system

Alternatively, you can use a simpler system, passing the ties through the holes in the mast, around the wind indicator / burgee and back out again, securing and adjusting them with simple, dependable and easily adjustable knots!

Boom outhaul system

Boom outhaul being adjusted while sailing

A strop spanning the middle half of the boom will reduce the boom bend but must not extend more than 10cm from the boom as this is the maximum the rules allow. The point where the mainsheet attaches to the strop is important. In light airs this needs to be just above the back of the daggerboard case. This allows you to keep your weight forward during tacks. In windier conditions the attachment point should be vertically above ratchet block. You can either have 2 separate rings or a single ring that can be slid along the strop. You can't move this attachment point while you are racing.

Boom strop for mainsheet attachment – here the attachment is forward, but it would move back in windier conditions

A boom uphaul loop (tack diagonal tie) must be fitted to the jaws. It slips over the pin on the front of the mast above the boom, controlling luff tension and length. To raise the boom and slacken the luff, simply twist the loop a few times before hooking it on.

Tack diagonal tie

Mainsheet

This should be attached to the boom strop with a quick-release clip. Only ball bearing blocks should be used. The upper becket block should attach to the clip with a length of dynema, to minimise the amount of mainsheet needed. The ratchet block must be dependable and the switch to engage the ratchet must not jam or slip. A lightweight sheet is best in light weather but beware of a freshening wind! Use or carry a pair of gloves. The purchase on the mainsheet is really down to sailor size.

3:1 mainsheet, suitable for larger sailors

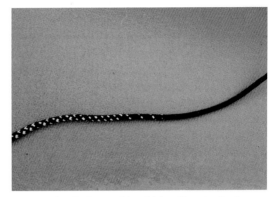

A tapered mainsheet, with a thicker diameter for the part you hold

Kicking Strap (Vang)

The kicking strap (vang) is usually made up of two ropes. An initial Dyneema rope from the boom to a loop through which a larger diameter, softer rope is attached and led through the cleat and wrapped over the boom to make it easier to use.

Change the softer rope regularly otherwise it will harden and wear at the cleating point.

For smaller sailors it is worth making the system 4:1

The 4:1 system can be rigged by tying or clipping the mainsheet to the becket to allow you to drop this down to a 3:1 in lighter winds.

Consider tapering the sheet but make sure the thicker part never gets to the ratchet block. You can even taper the far end of the sheet and tie it to the back of the toestrap to save weight and reduce the risk of knots in the mainsheet.

The kicking strap

Toestraps

Get the right position and tension. Tight straps maximise the rate of response of the boat to helm movement and reduce knee bend.

If you are bigger with longer legs, consider having toestraps which meet close behind the ratchet block to make them further from the gunwale. If you are small, make sure the toestraps are pulled out to the side of the boat so you can get your bottom over the side easily.

Have the toestraps held up by elastic so it's easy to slip your feet under them after a tack or gybe.

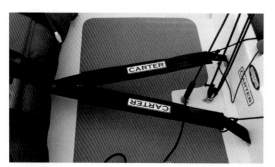

Toestraps for the smaller sailor, held up by elastic

Hiking Pants

Padded trousers or strap-on pads make hiking much more comfortable. They should not be worn in light weather as they make it harder for you to move easily and feel what the boat is doing. Also make sure there isn't too much of a bump at the edges of the pads as this can make sliding in and out difficult.

Painter

IOCA rules require at least 8m of 5mm buoyant rope. Attach to the mast foot, tie a loop 40cm up the line (on which to tie painters of boats being towed astern) and stow under a buoyancy strap amidships. Praddles, sandwiches, water bottles, and so on should all be stowed amidships and not in the ends of the boat.

Compass

A compass is not essential, but it can be a very useful tool when sailing at sea with few landmarks to help spot the shifts. The most popular is the spherical Silva compass.

The Silva is usually mounted on the vertical face of the mast thwart in the mid-line. It has a simple mounting bracket which enables it to be removed when not in use. It operates accurately at all angles of heel and has a magnified black card with a Degree Scale in white and a Tactical Scale in yellow.

The Tactical Scale is read behind the sight line nearest the windward side of the boat. The scale is designed so that, when the boat tacks through 90°, the difference between the readings on the two tacks is 10 – e.g. Port: 8; Starboard: 18.

On starboard tack, when the wind lifts and the boat points higher, the reading on the Tactical Scale decreases. When headed the reading increases. On port tack the opposite is true: when lifted the reading increases, when headed it decreases. Mark the sides of the bulkhead with a reminder! Note that each unit on the Tactical Scale is 18 degrees, so even a half unit shift is quite significant.

The popular spherical Silva compass

WIND & CURRENT

PART 4

CHAPTER 9

Seeing The Wind

With a bit of imagination, the wind can be visualised flowing over and around everything. It slips over water, jumping from wave top to wave top, with little eddies in the troughs. It is slowed and deflected by friction as it rubs over land and sea, mountains and forests, farmland and lakes. The wind finds the easiest route to flow around obstacles, just like water moving over rocks in a stream.

Imagine yourself sailing a course with headlands, moored ships, valley inlets and a patch of forest near the water. Use the wind bends to get to the windward mark first, and always sail towards the centre of a bend.

Feel the wind on your face. Is it blowing harder on one cheek than the other? Can you feel it on your ears? When it cools both sides equally, you are facing dead upwind. Hear the wind. Look upwind and move your head slowly from side to side. When you can hear it whistling equally in both ears, you are looking dead upwind.

See the wind on the water. You will see ripples being blown downwind. On smooth water these ripples are exactly at right angles to the surface wind. On rougher water you will see most ripples on the tops of waves where the wind strikes. As the surface wind varies, the ripples in each group will be from a slightly different direction, but they can still give a good overall indication of the wind direction.

On freshwater in strong winds, foamy lines can be seen going dead downwind on the water's surface. Seen from a height these can map out the airflow over a lake, showing wind bends.

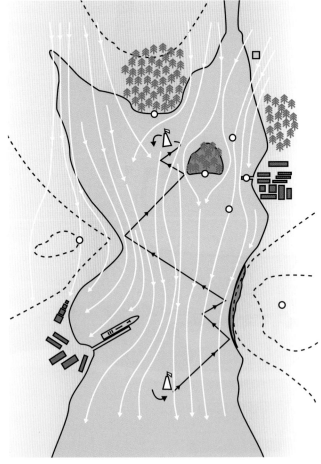

When sailing in an estuary or river you have to imagine how the wind blows over hills, through trees, or past ships lying at an angle to the wind; always sail towards the centre of a wind bend

Gusts

Gusts can be seen as dark patches on the water, with bigger waves sometimes breaking with white flashes of foam. Look at the patterns gusts make when they hit the water. First you see a dark circular patch where the gust strikes. Then dark lines run out from it in all directions as the supercharged wind explodes outwards. You may also see areas where there is consistently more wind, maybe where it is funnelling down a valley or accelerating around a headland.

In gusty weather keep an eye open to windward. When you see the tell-tale dark patch of a gust approaching, try to see which way it is moving:

- If it is moving head on towards you, the wind escaping from it will head you: tack and you will get an enormous lift.
- If the gust is to the side of you and moving towards you over your shoulder, as it hits you are likely to get a lift: be ready to head up and sit out hard!

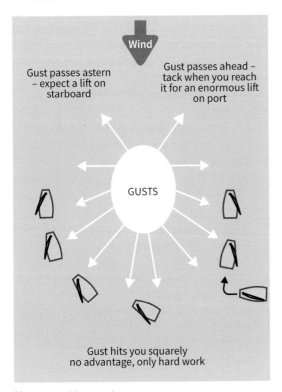

How to react to a gust

Anticipating The Wind

Besides looking at the course and imagining how the wind will blow over it, look at the clouds. The lower clouds are of vital importance in predicting the wind.

Cumulus clouds mean air is rising

Under a puffy white cumulus cloud the air is going up, so there will be less wind and it tends to back (shift to the left). As the cloud passes, faster air gusts down from the higher 'gradient' wind to replace the hot air rising in the cloud. This wind will be stronger and veered (shifted to the right). This shift effect would be reversed in the southern hemisphere.

So, as a cloud approaches, sail on port as the wind drops and goes left; after it passes, sail on starboard through the fresher veered wind. Look for gusts coming down through the blue gaps between these clouds (stronger and veered).

Dark rain clouds usually mean air is dropping

Dark clouds, which may have rain falling from them, are normally dropping cold air out of them. This will show as a gust or squall on the water. The gusts fan out from the cloud so, if the cloud is to the right of you, the wind will pull right and lift you on starboard. If the cloud is to the left of you, the lift will be on port.

Be careful; not all clouds are growing and sucking air up or reducing and dropping air down. A lot of clouds are fairly dormant, or are too high, and have little effect on the wind at ground level. So, try to use the cloud as an indicator but also look for the tell-tail signs of gusts on the water.

Sails Bending The Wind

Imagine the airflow around an Optimist sail when going upwind. A boat on the same tack to leeward or a little behind will be headed by the turned wind and will slow down. A boat close to the windward quarter will also be slowed down, both by striking the wash and by being headed by the deflected wind. A boat on the other tack crossing the stern of our boat will get a lift from the turned wind.

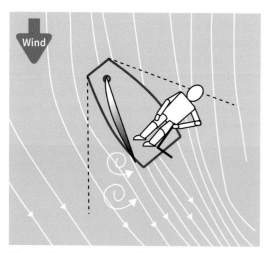

The wind being bent by a sail on the beat

If you are sailing in 'dirty wind' that has been deflected by someone else's sail, don't hesitate – tack and use the lift! Matters are much worse if you are in the dirty wind of several boats. This is the position when you are in the third rank at the start. It is essential that you get onto port tack and wriggle out, going under the starboard tack boats to the right-hand side of the course. Because of the turned wind from their sails you will be lifted or reaching, and hopefully eventually find some 'clean' air.

In team racing, when close covering, your aim is to get the opponent squarely in your backwind, tacking to keep covering him if he tacks. This will slow him down considerably, and he can be slowed even more if you oversheet as he loses speed. Don't slow down more than he does, or he will tack and go through you!

When reaching, the deflected wind will make it difficult for anybody to pass close to leeward, as several boats in a group will produce a big block of slow-moving deflected wind.

On the run, an Optimist throws a disturbed wind area ahead of it. This goes for different distances ahead depending on the wind strength. Groups of running boats produce very damaging areas of slow-moving turbulent wind to be avoided at all costs by boats ahead and by boats on the beat – never beat through groups of running boats: even if you avoid the wind shadow, the wash will get you!

Wind Theory

This is fascinating and essential knowledge for every sailor. Recommended reading is *Wind Strategy* by David Houghton and Fiona Campbell – also part of Fernhurst Books' *Sail to Win* series – which covers the following vitally important concepts:

*   Surface wind refraction
*   Stable and unstable air
*   Coastal effects
*   Convergence and divergence
*   Typical lake winds
*   How tide and water temperature changes affect the wind
*   Gusts and lulls, downdrafts and squalls
*   Sea breezes
*   Messages from the clouds
*   Obstacles in the wind

Windshift Sailing

By keeping awake and using windshifts you can sail a shorter course upwind, covering the distance to the weather mark more directly and leaving those fast guys who went the wrong way struggling far astern!

Spotting Shifts
- Watch your boat's heading on the shore ahead. When you are lifted you can point 'higher' up the shore; when backed 'lower'.
- Be sensitive to the adjustments you have to make, feeling when you have been able to point higher or have had to bear away a lot to stay on the wind.
- Watch the boats around you. If you seem to be getting lifted above the boats to leeward and the boats to windward are being lifted above you, you are on a lift. If the boats to leeward of you suddenly seem to be pulling ahead and you are dropping down, while the boats to windward drop towards you, you are being headed!
- Watch clouds, wind on the water, boats to windward.
- Use your compass.

Getting To Know The Wind Pre-Start
You need to find out:
- Wind shifts expected during the race, due to meteorological changes or sea breezes. The expected shifts can be worked out in advance from the weather forecast and inspired guesswork on the morning of the race.
- Wind bends on the course. Are these likely? Look at a map of the area. If you think there is a possibility of a wind bend, then agree with your buddy to check it with a split tack before the start.
- When at the course, sail upwind and check the frequency of oscillation of the wind. Wind is seldom steady, oscillating from side to side with a frequency that may be as short as 30 seconds or as long as 30 minutes. By sailing the beat, you should get an idea of how many times you will have to tack to stay on the lifted tack.
- While you are doing this practice beat, try to find the mean wind direction and how large the shifts are. If you use a compass this will be a lot more precise. Look at the gusts and areas of stronger wind. Is there any pattern to them? Is there more wind in certain areas of the course or are gusts lifting more on one tack?

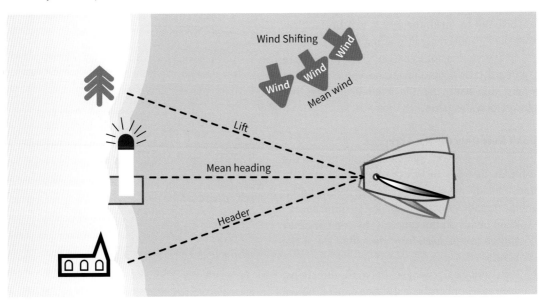

Watch your boat's heading when sailing towards the shore or a fixed object

Use The Compass

Avoid using a compass until you are happy sailing an Optimist fast and accurately and you are comfortable sailing on shifts using feel, other boats and where you are heading on a shoreline. Once you reach this level of competence then a compass can be a valuable tool. Before that it can be a distraction.

Once in the start area, sail upwind on one tack for ten minutes or so checking the frequency of oscillation and the maximum lift and maximum header. From these you can work out the mean wind direction and the compass settings / readings that represent the mean upwind course on each tack.

The importance of this is that, when you are on a lift and the wind starts to back slowly, you must be careful not to tack until the wind and your upwind course have swung 'back' past the mean direction. In very shifty weather, if you lose sight of the mean headings on each tack you will be tacking on small headers and losing out badly.

After the start it is easy to glance at the compass to check that you are sailing on, or higher than, the mean upwind course for that tack without loss of concentration on speed. If you see that you are heading below the mean course, then take the first opportunity to tack! The result will be faultless shift sailing and a magnificent first mark position!

Of course, it is not as easy as this. Not only are starboard tack boats preventing you from going where you want, but the wind itself does not always 'play the game'.

Don't Rely Only On The Compass

Use your eyes as well. You can only depend on the compass for your tactics in winds that oscillate from a steady mean direction. Do not blindly sail on compass readings in the following circumstances:

- Wind bends on the course. (The compass may still be useful away from the influence of the bend.)
- Meteorological changes in wind directions, such as a front crossing the race area or the sea breeze coming in. Such wind direction changes

will make nonsense of mean wind estimates. If you do not spot that the wind is changing permanently, and take it to be just a good lift, you will end up sailing on a long, slowly lifting tack when it would have been better to take a short hitch towards the new wind direction and then lay the mark. Keep a good eye on boats to windward. What wind have they got? Where is it coming from? When the wind steadies again, by all means reset your compass but be cautious about trusting it absolutely.

- If the frequency of oscillation of the wind is longer than the duration of the windward leg, you will sail one beat on one part of the wind cycle and the next beat on another part. In these circumstances your compass is of little value except to give an idea of where you are in the cycle.

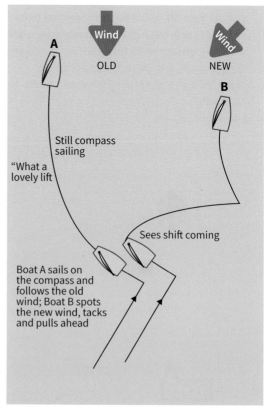

Don't rely only on the compass – get your head out of the boat and look for major changes to the wind

CHAPTER 10

Understanding Current

A great number of venues you will race at will have current caused either by tide, river flow or the wind. This can be very confusing for sailors, especially if they normally sail inland.

The first thing to do is to research the venue. Is it likely to have current? Look on the internet to find tide tables. This will give you the high and low water times and the rise and fall of the water. Consider any river flows by looking at Google Maps. Or is it a big expanse of water that might have wind-driven current?

Is the current likely to be the same across the whole of the course or is it likely to vary? If it is going to be different across the course, you may be able to use the current to your advantage or there might be only one way to go that will pay.

Current Uniform Across Course

Let's assume the current is going to be uniform across the whole course for the race. This means that, as long as you stay inside the laylines upwind and sail a straight-line course between the marks downwind, you can concentrate on your normal wind and boat tactics – tacking on shifts, sailing into gusts and avoiding dirty air.

This sounds easy but many sailors get this wrong and overstand marks, sail big loops down reaches and on the wrong gybe down the run.

Let's think about the main factors to consider depending which way the current is flowing relative to the course / wind.

Wind Against Current
- Beware being over the start line. The current is pushing you over. Get a good transit and don't get on the line too early.

- The beat will feel shorter and you will need to tack before the usual laylines as the current is pushing you up towards the windward mark.
- The waves will be steeper and closer together than normal. Be prepared to modify your technique to cope with this.
- You can shoot the windward mark since the current is pushing you up, so a late tack in can be a good tactical move.
- The run will feel longer as you sail into the current and the fleet will be very close and bunch up as it rounds the windward mark. The big priority is to try to keep your air clear.
- Make your turn late on the leeward marks since you will have to be careful not to get swept into them by the current

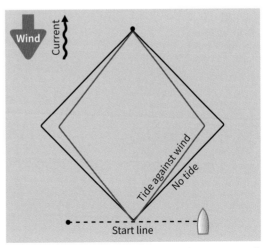

With wind against current, the beat will feel shorter and you need to tack earlier for the laylines

- Try not to get pushed high on the reach by the current else you will end up running into the mark with the tide against you. Not very fast! Use a front or back transit to sail the direct line. If there is no transit, look at both marks to make a judgement as to whether you are still sailing the direct route.

Wind With Current

- The current is pushing you back from the start line. Get a good transit and don't get too far away from the line. You will have to keep sailing to stay on the line. There is often a big line sag in the middle of the line. The beat will feel longer, and you will need to overstand the normal laylines as the current is pushing you down.
- Beware of getting too close to the windward mark. The current is pushing you onto it. Never try to shoot the windward mark.
- The run will feel shorter as you sail with the current. This will mean that the fleet will spread out as it rounds the windward mark. Try to stay in the middle of the run else the current will sweep you past the mark and you will end up reaching to get to it.
- Make your turn early on the leeward marks since you will have to be careful not to get

swept past them by the current
- Try not to get pushed low on the reach by the current or else you will end up beating into the mark with the tide against you. Not very fast! Use a front or back transit to sail the direct line. If there is no transit, look at both marks to make a judgement as to whether you are still sailing the direct route.

Current Across The Wind

- The current will be pushing you towards one end of the start line. Beware of starting at the end the current is pushing to. It is very easy to get there too early, then you will end up in a raft on the pin or the committee boat.
- The beat will probably have a long and a short tack. Watch your laylines – one you will have to tack earlier on, the other you will need to overstand.
- Be aware of the current flow on the windward mark – it will either be pushing you hard onto it or sweeping you past it.
- The run will have the tide across it, so it is likely to have a favoured gybe for the whole run. Try to get a transit on the leeward mark and sail a straight line to the mark.
- If the leeward mark is a gate think about which mark is better for the current. Will you get

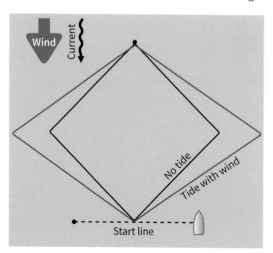

With wind with current, the beat will feel longer and you need to tack for the laylines later

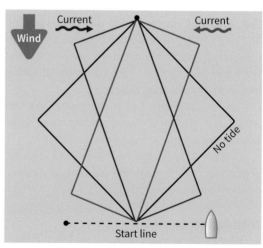

With wind across current, if the windward mark is laid directly upwind, one tack will be longer

caught in a leebow from another boat when you round the mark or will the boat in front get swept wide and open up a lane for you.

- The reach will either have the current behind you or you will be sailing into it. If sailing into it, this will close the fleet up and make the reach feel a lot longer. The opposite is true if the current is behind you.

Current Varying Across The Course

The current can vary in strength or direction across the course. If this is the case, the important factor is to ensure you sail in the least adverse current or the strongest advantageous current.

How can you predict where the current is strongest or where the direction might change?

Venturi Effect
This is the effect where the flow of water increases as it is squeezed or compressed through a gap such as between a shoreline and an island.

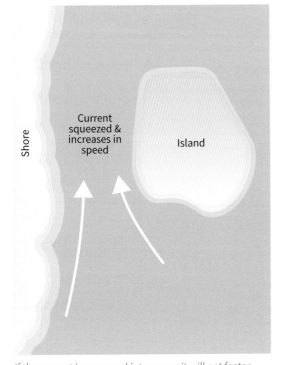

If the current is squeezed into a gap, it will get faster

It could be that it is just compressed trying to get around a headland. Remember this will also cause a change in direction of the flow. In extreme circumstances a headland can cause the flow to sweep around it and then swirl into a reversed flow (a back eddy).

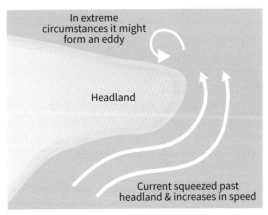

The current can be compressed going around a headland – which will also change its direction and possibly cause eddies

Shallow Water
Current flows slower in shallow water because of the friction with the sea or riverbed. So, if current is flowing along the shoreline, it is likely to be slower inshore and faster out to sea.

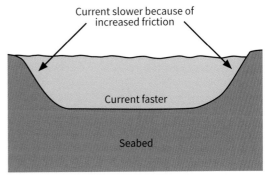

The current flows slower in shallow water

However, if a current is passing over a shallow bank it will speed up because of the Venturi effect mentioned above. So be careful, not all shallow water is slower moving!

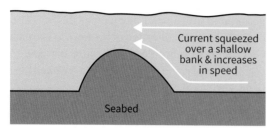

The Venturi effect can happen over a shallow bank, increasing the speed of the current

Bends Around Land

Current will try to take the easiest route around shorelines or islands. This will bend the current direction and might mean the current is different at the top of the course to the bottom.

Once you have predicted how the current will be flowing on the course it is important that you check exactly what it is doing on the course.

A good visual clue as to changes in current strength or direction are tide lines. Where different current flows meet you will probably see either a disturbance in the wave pattern, a difference in water colour or maybe a line of seaweed or rubbish floating in the water.

To tell the direction and strength of the current look at any fixed objects such as a mark, lobster pot or the anchored committee boat. Look at how the water is flowing around it.

To be more accurate use a sponge or an almost full water bottle and throw it into the water next to the object. How far does it drift in one minute and in what direction? Don't forget to retrieve your bottle or sponge!

This is where your coach can also be useful. They should have a tide stick so they can get readings around the course and feed them back to you before the start. This will help you make the best strategic and tactical decisions about the current.

You can see the direction and strength of the current against a buoy

A change in the water surface can show a change in the current

PART 5

CHAPTER 11

Mental Fitness

In the top of any national squad you tend to find accomplished and experienced sailors who have good boat handling skills, knowledge of tactics and the racing rules, race-prepared boats with good sails, and the ability to sail fast.

Why is it, then, that certain people win nearly all the time?

Why Some People Win

Objective Evaluation

Winners are able to evaluate their own feelings and performance before, during and after competition. They develop the ability to examine their performance, identify strong and weak points (through using approaches described in this chapter), and then use that knowledge to plan changes in tactics or training to correct matters. They are also capable of identifying damaging emotions before, during or after a competition. They have a 'growth mindset' attitude.

Clear Planning

Winners are able to set achievable training goals covering specific processes which require work (e.g. bailing to windward). They set performance goals (e.g. sail the beat perfectly; plan tactics for every situation), and also set outcome goals (e.g. win a race in the Nationals, top ten in the Worlds).

Highly Confident

Winners are totally confident of their ability. They are sure they can sail a perfect race, and winning or not winning is subject only to the vagaries of the sport. They have perfected techniques to maintain their confidence and block out failures.

Stress Management

Winners are aware of their levels of stress and can use techniques to keep that level optimum for top performance. If you are too stressed, or too laid-back, performance suffers.

Mental Rehearsal

Winners are able to visualise their sailing so effectively that they can practise starts, mark roundings and other tactical manoeuvres without going afloat.

Visualise surfing down a wave so you get it right on the water

Winners have a developed ability to visualise each different part of the race, to examine it and the emotions felt at that time. You can use visualisation techniques to come to terms with a race in which you made a major error by visualising a successful outcome. If you lost your cool at a particular time in a race, you could visualise the lead-up to the incident, trying to pinpoint exactly what threw you.

Concentration

Winners have developed the ability to concentrate deeply for long periods.

In addition, a characteristic of Olympic competitors is their strong will to win. To excel at that standard of competition, strong motivation is essential. These competitors have the overpowering ambition to be 'better than all the rest'. They don't want to lose, but must avoid the negative fear of losing. This drives them to try harder, hike further and longer, concentrate more, sail accurately and carefully, think fast, keep mentally calm, stay physically flexible, and work!

Winners are driven to try harder, hike further and longer and concentrate more

Mental Tools

Training & Racing Log

As an aid to self-coaching, on the evening after a race day, thoughtfully and honestly fill in a Race Analysis Sheet (p116).

The most important entries will not be mast rake, sail used or foil rake, but your assessment of your performance. What went well and what aspects of your sailing need more work?

The next step is to do something about it! Keep these sheets in your log and, as you achieve your training and medium term goals, your confidence will improve with your results.

Scrapbook

Keep this for results, pictures, sailing instructions and so on and, when you've had a bad day, thumb through and see how much you have improved and remember your good races.

Keep a 'scalp' page and enter the name of every top sailor you beat. If you can beat them once you can do it again! Keep notes of anything you learnt or interesting information.

Keep a log of your performances

Video

If you've had a good race or series, try to get a copy of a video of it. Every time you watch it you will get a confidence boost. It will also help you visualise yourself sailing well.

Talk

Take every chance to talk to top sailors about how they've achieved their successes, and imagine yourself in their shoes.

'30 Second Bubble'

This is a useful way of coping with things that happen during a race. Shut out anything that has happened over 30 seconds ago. Concentrate only on the present and immediate future as if you are in a bubble of time.

The bubble will help you exclude from your mind everything that has or will happen outside that time. Forget the hassle; let it go, settle down, control yourself and get back to concentrating on simply sailing fast!

Look Forward & Out

This is another useful coping technique. If something happens, try to forget it by concentrating hard on sailing your boat fast purely by feel, keeping your eyes forward and out, scanning only the water immediately ahead and to leeward until you have control again.

If something goes wrong, look forward and out

Examine Your Emotions

An example is fear. What are you afraid of exactly? Is it a logically justified fear? Is it stiffening your muscles or interfering with your breathing? Fear is a natural safety mechanism, making you 'freeze'.

It's natural; you can't do anything about it; so accept it but be firm that you are not going to let it rule you or interfere with your race.

Desensitisation To Aggravating Factors

If you get up-tight when people shout, get all the other members of your training group to shout during exercises. After coping with friendly shouting, strangers shouting in competition will not be so daunting.

Similarly, competitors have to learn to accept decisions of 'on the water judges', however inept or wrong they may seem at the time. This can be practised by introducing a number of unjust and erroneous rulings into training that competitors have to accept.

Self-Affirmation & Buzz Words

Look in the mirror on race day, look yourself in the eye, and say "You're good – you've beaten them all before". Say "Great!" when things go right, "Good tack!" when you do a good one, "Slippery!" as you slide swiftly downwind. When you pull off a cunning move, say "Sneaky!", "Another one bites the dust!", or something similar. It will keep you hyped up and flying. Build up a selection of buzz words to use at different times in the race.

Arousal

If you are feeling lethargic after a postponement or waiting around between starts, force yourself to begin checking the wind and your boat set-up, and practise some boat handling. This should get you more focussed.

Controlled Aggression

This can be effective afloat in getting your own way. In using this technique, it is essential that you can keep your mind cool and clear, and do not infringe the rules. Be very careful that you do not show bad sportsmanship and unfair sailing (RRS 2) or 'commit an act of misconduct' (RRS 69). This clearly excludes the use of bad language and bullying in your dealings with other competitors.

Assertiveness

Sailors need to develop assertiveness, based on a sound knowledge of the rules. A loud and clear early hail of "Protest" can work wonders. Don't let the aggressive kids have it all their own way!

Singing & Whistling

These are good for you when racing. They help you relax and distract the opposition. The secret is to develop the ability to do them without thinking about it!

Executioner's Eye, Gunslinger's Smile

This is a phrase from a book by Dennis Conner who won the America's Cup four times. It is useful when in tactical battles with an opponent. It is also handy in helping you counter the psyching-out and winding-up talk that goes on in the dinghy park at big events.

If somebody is trying to get you worried, give him the gunslinger's smile and look him over for execution!

Ten Things That Require Zero Talent

While much of this book is about the skills and techniques which determine your sailing talent, there are a lot of things which can help your sailing which require no talent – just the right attitude. Here are the commonly quoted top ten:

1. **Punctuality**
2. **Work ethic**
3. **Effort**
4. **Body language**
5. **Energy**
6. **Attitude**
7. **Passion**
8. **Being coachable**
9. **Doing extra**
10. **Being prepared**

Have these attitudes and your sailing talent will go further!

Be assertive, particularly in close situations

CHAPTER 12

The Perfect Body

Heavy Or Lightweight?

Weight is of great interest to Optimist sailors and their parents! Usually they have no need to worry, for the Optimist is a remarkably weight-tolerant boat. An experienced heavyweight can confound opinion and turn in winning performances in all weathers. A demonstration of this was given by Ben Ainslie at the 1992 UK National Championship, which he dominated in both light and heavy weather, weighing 63kg (10 stone). Although this was a long time ago, and it was Ben, it is still applicable.

For average sailing conditions the optimum sailing weight would probably be 35-56kg (6-8st), but each weight group has its own particular problems of rig tune, trim, movement in the boat and technique which have to be solved for top performance.

Physical Development

Optimist sailing spans late childhood and early adolescence. During this time the steady growth of childhood leads into the 'growth spurt', a two-year period of very rapid height gain, after which growth slows down as adult height is reached. Individuals develop at very different rates: early developers may be physically up to four years ahead of their peers in height and strength, but their growth stops earlier. By 18 they have often been passed by guys who were the smallest in the class at the age of 12!

In the Optimist class it is common to see these well-co-ordinated and strong early developers dominating the younger age groups, but they can get too big and heavy in their final Optimist year. By this time their later-maturing friends are getting stronger and are reaching optimum weight.

The Optimist can be sailed by lightweights and heavyweights

Growth Risks

Identifying the growth spurt is important because, during this time, the mechanical advantage of muscle groups change, making an individual much more susceptible to injury. This problem can be seen most clearly in some thin children who go through an awkward clumsy phase during their growth spurt, when the bones seem to grow faster than the muscle needed to move them and the nervous system's ability to control them.

All young athletes in training are particularly at risk of sustaining injury to the growing bone ends, ligaments and muscles when exercising strenuously. The most common and well-known problem for sailors (as for footballers) is Osgood Schlatter's Syndrome, a painful swelling on the upper end of the tibia where the patella tendon attaches to the growing area of bone. Hiking hard (or kicking a heavy football) can lead to strain and considerable inflammation at this point, as the muscular action of the quadriceps tries to pull the tendon off the bone. The treatment is rest and no hiking (or kicking) until it settles, sometimes for six months!

Boys & Girls

Adolescence in boys brings a sharp increase in height, weight, shoulder width, muscle, bone mass and strength. They become leaner, losing the body fat of childhood. Boys have the peak of their growth spurt around about the age of 14, but it can be as early as 12 or as late as 16. Adult height is usually reached at about 17 or 18.

In girls, adolescence brings first an increase in height, followed some six months later by a weight increase. Their strength does increase at this time, but much less than the boys and most of the weight gain is in fat rather than muscle. Girls have their growth spurt peak around the age of 12, though it may be as early as 10 or as late as 14. By 15 to 16 a girl will normally have reached full adult height.

In the final Opi year (aged 15) girls have had their growth spurt and strength gain, without the full weight gain of late teen years. Boys on the other hand are in the middle of their growth and have not yet developed the muscle of later years. It is thus still possible for boys and girls to compete equally.

Puberty and an increase in hormone levels can cause physical, mood and behavioural changes in adolescent children as well as mental and emotional preoccupation. The onset of menstruation must be treated sympathetically, but it need not necessarily affect performance in training and competition.

Boys and girls can compete against each other in Optimists

CHAPTER 13

Physical Fitness

Physical fitness is seldom necessary for successful performance at club level, but becomes increasingly important for good results at regional, national and international levels.

Fitness Helps

Fitness can help your sailing in four main ways:

1. It helps to prevent you from getting tired. Racing, particularly in heavy weather, can be exhausting. If you are fit, you will be able to sail harder and keep fighting longer than the next sailor. This will have you moving up the leaderboard.

2. It speeds up your recovery between races. The demands of championship sailing are often much greater than those encountered in a single event. Incomplete recovery between races held 'back to back' or on successive days can lead to you getting more and more tired, and less capable of doing your best in the races at the end of a hard series. Avoid this by being physically fit.

3. It keeps you sharp mentally. Tired, unfit sailors find concentration difficult. This affects their ability to make quick correct tactical decisions, and their performance suffers. Physical exhaustion makes it much harder to keep mentally positive and cope emotionally with events during the race. The fitter you are the better you will perform mentally.

4. It prevents injuries. Most injuries occur when the body is tired and cold. When you are fit, you are much less likely to injure yourself when racing hard. Minimise injuries by being fit and more able to withstand what competing throws at you.

Training Requirements

Size & Weight

Training requirements vary with a competitor's size. Sailors weighing less than 35kg should aim to develop stamina, hiking and arm strength. Sailors weighing over 50kg need to develop flexibility, agility, balance and coordination, although stamina is still needed in heavy weather.

Time On The Water

Hours on the water can, of course, make a useful contribution to fitness. If you could sail three times a week for an hour or more in winds of force 4 or above, you would certainly develop good sailing fitness. However, it is impractical for most Optimist sailors to do this even if the wind were suitable. In the summer only 30% of days in Britain have winds of this strength or more. More winter days have suitable winds but, with a winter race training programme, extra stamina and fitness training is needed. This can be provided by sport and fun in and out of school:

- Flexibility: Stretching and warm-up exercises
- Balance: Surfing; windsurfing; skateboarding; wiggle boarding
- Agility: Football; rugby; hockey; netball
- Co-ordination and reactions: Badminton; table tennis; tennis; squash; golf
- Strength: Circuits or rugby training
- Stamina: Distance running; jogging; cycling; swimming

Warm-Up & Flexibility

Warming-Up

Warming-up before training and exercise avoids injuring cold muscles and ligaments. Ideally you should warm-up and warm-down before and after all strenuous sailing. Before races it is often worth warming-up twice – on shore and just after the orange flag is displayed. After general recalls or a postponement a warm-up routine can not only help the muscles but will also help to wake you up and get you ready to fight.

Flexibility

This refers to the range of movement which is possible at joints. You need a fair amount of flexibility to move around a boat smoothly and easily. Some girls have most amazing natural flexibility, while some boys, particularly the muscular early developers, can be remarkably stiff.

Flexibility can be improved by regular gentle stretching exercises. For these to be effective, the end of the range of movement must be reached and the position held for a few seconds. It is important that such exercises are always carried out in a controlled manner. Violent, rapid or bouncing movements should be avoided as these are likely to be ineffective and may lead to injury.

First Warm-Up: Flexibility

2. Arm circling: 15 forward, 15 back

3. Back flexion stretch: Lying on back with knees bent; draw right knee and nose together using hands to help: repeat with left knee, then both knees

4. Quadriceps stretch: Lie on front, bend left knee; reach behind with the left hand, hold left foot, bring it to buttock, and increase stretch so that knee just rises from floor: repeat with right

1. Running on the spot: 1 minute; or **Step-ups**: 15 leading with right leg, 15 with left

5. Shoulder stretch: *Standing feet astride, hands in front of chest, arms horizontal, press elbows backwards then forwards*

6. Trunk twist with head turning: *Start as for shoulder stretch; rotate trunk and head to left; repeat to right*

7. Side bend: *Standing, feet shoulder-width apart, press one hand on hip while stretching the opposite arm over the head at 45°: repeat other side*

8. Sitting stretch: *Sitting with both legs outstretched, gradually lean forwards from the hips – do not push towards the feet by rounding the back and leading with the head, as this can cause back strain*

9. Back extension stretch: *Lie on the floor face down with hands palm down under the shoulders, and forearms alongside trunk; push up the trunk keeping the hips on the floor; relax in this position, then slowly lower*

Warming Up Afloat

It is good practice to get afloat well before the start of the race in order to check conditions, decide how to play the first beat, set the boat up for the winds found on the course, check out the favoured end of the start line, and so on. However, being on the water early and not being very active can mean that the body becomes quite cold by the time the race is due to start. This can be even more of a problem if races are postponed or there are recalls. A short 'warm-up' can help a lot!

Usually you would want to do this just after the orange flag gets displayed. If there are recalls or postponements, repeat if you are starting to feel cold.

Here are some things you could try for one or two minutes:

2. Running on the spot

1. Rapid shadow boxing *with a circling rather a jerking movement.*

3. Arm circling, *forward or backward*

4. Hand and neck circling, *in both directions*

5. Press-ups, *with arms on transom or gunwale*

You could also do a practice sail and throw in 10 tacks then bear away and do 5 gybes. This has the added advantage of getting you focused on the conditions again.

A Sailor's Circuit

For those of you who want to go for the Olympics in ten years, and for folks who can't stand school sport, here is a 'Circuit' that you can do a number of times a week at home. It incorporates exercises for your back and hiking muscles. Make sure you warm-up and stretch before starting the circuit.

Find your exercise targets by performing each of the exercises for 30 seconds and record your scores, taking a 1-minute rest between each exercise. Next session, go through the exercises in turn, doing each exercise the target number of times. Repeat the sequence three times over. Time yourself and note it down. Each time you do the circuit, try to improve your score.

1. Quadriceps: *Stand on one leg with the other bent to a right angle at the knee. You can hold onto something if it helps. Bend the weight-bearing leg slowly, by about 20° only. Hold for 1 second. Then straighten the leg again. Repeat 5 times, then change legs.*

2. Running on the spot: *Use vigorous arm movements. Lift feet about 10cm (4in) off the floor. Count each time the left foot touches down.*

3. Back extensor: *Lie on stomach. Keeping the knees straight, lift one leg while keeping the hips in contact with the ground. Hold in the air for a moment then slowly lower. Repeat 5 times, then change legs.*

4. Sit-ups with twist: Lying on your back with fingers holding ear lobes and knees bent to 90°, sit up to touch knee with opposite elbow.

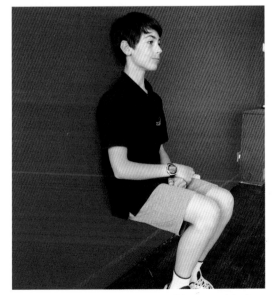

5. Wall sits: With knees and hips well bent to 90°, 'sit' with back against a wall and arms folded without sagging for 30 seconds.

6. Back flexor / abdominal strengthening: Lie on back, knees bent 90° with feet flat on the floor and not under a bar or bench. Hands on ears, tighten abdominal muscles, keep lower back flat, slowly raise head and shoulders off the floor until in half sitting position. Then slowly lower to starting position. Breathe out on raising and breathe in on lowering.

7. Walk around your feet: Start in press-up position and using arms only 'walk' in a circle around your feet. If you don't have room for a full circle, go from side to side through 90° and count the 'cycles'.

8. Press-ups: Ensure you hold your body straight and your arms go down to 90°.

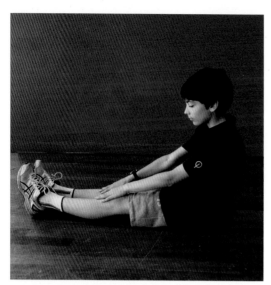

9. Isometric medial quadriceps: *Sit with legs straight, hands placed just above kneecaps. Contract quads, particularly the part on the inside of the thigh. Count to 5, then relax.*

10. Step-ups: *On to a stout chair or bench. Step up with one foot, follow with the other foot, lower first foot to floor, bring the other foot down, repeat.*

Stamina

To build up stamina you should aim to jog, run, cycle or swim for at least 20 minutes three times a week. A fanatic could try an 'Aerobic Trail':

- Jog – 5 minutes
- Squat thrusts – 30 seconds
- Run at half speed – 2 minutes
- Press-ups – 30 seconds
- Run fast 100m, jog 100m – 2 minutes
- Bent knee sit-ups – 30 seconds
- Run at half speed – 2 minutes
- Run on the spot, high knee raise – 30 seconds
- Run at half speed – 2 minutes
- Run fast 100m, jog 100m – 2 minutes
- Jog – 2 minutes

Hiking

There was a high incidence of knee problems when most sailors hiked draped over the gunwale with knees bent and body in an 'S' shape. It has been demonstrated that hiking 'Laser style', with knees bent no more than 20°, is less likely to cause knee injury. This is because the sideways pull of the main quadriceps muscle is balanced when the knee is straight by the pull of the medial quadriceps muscle. This muscle ceases to work effectively when the knee is bent more than 20°. The result is that the kneecap slips outwards and rubs on the outer ridge of the femur, causing wear and pain.

Try to hike like Laser sailors. Set your straps tight and high in the boat and sit out with knees bent no more than 20°. With practice this will be no more agonising than hiking in an S-shape, and you will have the benefit of being further from the water and less likely to be hit by waves. The special exercises for the medial quadriceps (circuit No.1 and No.9) are well worth doing.

Do not train with weights! While your back is growing as the ends of the bones are soft. Using weights in training can permanently damage your back, leading to back pain and weakness for the rest of your life.

Hiking correctly with knees bent no more than 20°

Eating For Energy, Fluid For Fitness

Energy is stored in your body as something called glycogen. It is important to have as much of this as possible in your body when you arrive at a major competition.

In The Week Before The Competition:

1. Eat plenty of complex carbohydrates – bread, cereals, spaghetti, rice, potatoes, beans, peas, lentils, root vegetables, fruit (bananas are brilliant), biscuits, cereal, muesli bars, cakes, puddings, sweet and fruit yoghurts, fruit juice. This will top your energy supply up as you near the event.
2. Cut down your training.
3. Avoid large meals. Eat little and often and increase your fluid intake.

At The Regatta

Before the regatta, find an 'energy bar' that you like and take enough to save the need for shopping. Chocolate bars contain mostly 'simple carbohydrates' and only give a short boost and should be avoided. Muesli bars are much better.

On the night before the regatta, have a good meal well before going to bed.

On the morning of the regatta, have a high carbohydrate breakfast with plenty of fluids. Complex carbohydrates are best. Allow yourself several hours to digest food properly before racing starts. Avoid being tempted by a big fry-up which is mostly protein with little energy value.

If the start is late, then consider an extra pasta pot mid-morning.

Try to eat simply during the regatta. Choose foods you are used to, avoid shellfish and undercooked or spicy food, and drink plenty of fluids.

Make sure you eat something and drink something between every race even if you don't feel hungry or thirsty.

Drink

During the event, and in training, sip fluid regularly. Before competing, drink 250-500ml of cold water; urine formation is reduced during exercise so 'pit stops' will not be necessary. At hot venues you will perspire more and will need to drink more. Avoid salt tablets – you don't need them – and isotonic high calorie drinks for sailing events, because they cause a surge of blood sugar that can increase your production of urine. Stick to water, weak squash or dilute fruit juices.

Eat and drink something before every race

After Races

Take fluid and some carbohydrates, preferably 'complex', starting as soon as possible after the race finishes. At the end of the day's racing, start refuelling immediately with a complex carbohydrate to give the glycogen stores as long as possible to build up. On coming ashore, the feeding process will continue.

On The Way To The Venue

Often to get from home to an event involves a long car journey or maybe even a ferry or flight.

If possible, arrive in plenty of time the night before an event so you have time to relax and recover.

On the journey try to keep active – play games or chat. Don't forget to eat and drink while you are travelling. Ideally prepare good healthy food before the journey. It's too easy to stop at a service station and buy unhealthy snacks!

Using your phone or watching films in the car can help make the journey pass, but it's a really good idea to switch them off half an hour before you arrive at the venue. Start chatting for the final half hour and start your mental preparation for the event – visualising it.

> **TOP TIP**
>
> In the final half hour of your journey, go through what you are going to do at the venue: what the day's going to be like, what you will be doing about food and so on. Use this valuable time for mental rehearsal so you are ready to go once you arrive!

Seasickness

There are a number of ways you can prevent seasickness:

1. Take seasickness tablets. Try different kinds at home until you find one that doesn't make you feel ill. Take them in the dose and at the times described in the information sheets.
2. Take sweets with you and suck regularly – barley sugar, peppermint, glucose.
3. Keep busy, keep sailing, particularly if you start feeling tired which is one of the first signs of trouble. Don't just stop and bob up and down!
4. Between races, stand up and keep your eye on the horizon rather than on the waves or the tossing boat.
5. Keep warm – cold people are sick quicker! Do onboard warm-up exercises.
6. Think positive. 'Great weather for surfing!', 'I can hack this!', 'Let's get down to work!'; not 'Yuk! I hate this. I'm going to be sick soon!'.
7. If all else fails, you can be sick and win yacht races. Many of the best sailors feel uneasy in a confused sea, but they don't let it beat them. Chuck up and get on with the race! Keep your mind on the job and don't let it damage your efficiency and resolve to race effectively.

PARENTS & COACHES

PART 6

CHAPTER 14

For Parents

A Push Too Far?

We all know the popularly-held image of the Optimist parent, towering over a crying child on the slipway, shouting "I told you to go left up the beat!". Of course, the vast majority of Optimist parents are not like that, but the few that are give the rest a bad name. We all want our child to do well and we get excited when they succeed and downhearted when something goes wrong. The average parent at a regatta:

1. Is ambitious for their child's success
2. Has invested heavily in gear, clothing, petrol and accommodation, and has spent many weekends doing nothing except follow the Optimist circuit
3. Can think of a list of things he or she could be doing elsewhere
4. Is unable to see what's happening afloat, and is cheered then depressed by garbled progress reports from those parents with high powered binoculars
5. In general, feels their child could and should do better

Obligation & Failure

None of the above points will help the child be a better sailor, but they can give the child feelings of obligation and failure, adding to the stress of competitive dinghy racing. The young sailor in question may be ambitious and talented, or of average ability and motivation. He or she may sail for a number of reasons that have not occurred to the parents:

- Independence afloat
- Because friends sail
- Good fun messing about in boats
- Been pushed into it by parents, but would much rather 'Listen to music, get onto my computer, go riding, play mini Rugby'

The Reasons Why

As parents we must look at why we take our children sailing. Is it frustrated ambition on our part, or because we feel we have something worthwhile to pass on to the child? We can seek to inspire our children with our enthusiasm and delight in sailing but have to allow them to find it for themselves. They are at an impressionable age

Good Optimist Parent	Bad Optimist Parent
Wants their child to enjoy sailing	Wants their child to win at all costs
Lets their child learn & make mistakes	Over controls their child
Lets their child have fun	Creates a pressurised atmosphere
Lets their child make decisions	Tells their child what to do
Praises their child	Criticises their child
Respects & supports the coach	Criticises & argues with the coach

and will certainly do what we want them to do, but the time will come when they will lose interest in the sport if they are not finding their own reasons to continue with it.

We must be sensitive to our children's attitude to competition, and to their aims in sailing and their everyday lives. Very few people are able to win national and international championships or the Olympics. We must support our children at the standard they wish to compete at, rather than constantly implying that they should be doing better than they are.

Parental Support

There are a few key elements of support that we can provide our children:
- Physical: Home, security, accommodation
- Emotional: Understanding, insight, comforting, supportive, loving father / mother figures, dependable, predictable, consistent, realistic, and inspirational
- Financial: Funding for boats, equipment, clothing, travel, accommodation, entry fees
- Logistical: Transport to home club for training, open meetings, national and international events, arranging accommodation, feeding afloat and ashore
- Bosun: Checking, repair, maintenance, launching and landing assistance
- Facilitator: All the time

Parents can help and support without taking over

A Bad Result

Don't start listing what went wrong as soon as they come ashore. Let them do the talking if they want to; if they don't, try to avoid discussion of events until emotions have cooled. Try to work out your child's recovery time. After a bad race, competitors of all ages need a time to recover emotionally, before being able to think clearly and analytically.

Give some thought to your reaction to seeing them sail the worst race of their life. How long do you need to recover before you can:
- Be civil to anybody?
- Bring yourself to look at the child?
- Speak to the child?
- Control your body language (hunched shoulders, glowering face, irritable movements)?
- Discuss the race objectively, without your disappointment being transferred to the child?

The Child's View

Your child may well know more about sailing than you will ever do and will certainly know more about what happened afloat. They may be bitterly disappointed by their result, know that you will be disappointed, and will feel wretched before you utter a word. In such circumstances some young sailors do not want to come ashore to face their parents' reaction.

Try not to say a word; give them a squeeze and put their boat away. Later that night, after relaxing and eating, you will both be in a better frame of mind to take a logical and realistic look at the situation. Show them that whatever happens you love them and think they are great!

Treat them in the same way whether they win or lose and try to act naturally on the drive home even after a total disaster. Do be sensitive to their needs, and considerate of their moods. Give your child space to develop as an independent person. Try to work out what your child really feels about competing – is it just to please you? Praise and emphasise the good things your child did in the racing. Build up their self-esteem and beware the careless comment that may put them down.

- Do have realistic aspirations for your child
- Don't use sarcasm at any time
- Do encourage your children to take part in other sports
- Don't fall out openly with other parents, or upset your child's opponents
- Let the coach do the coaching; do not undermine him or her

Parents With Coaching Ability

Be careful not to limit your child's ability to use his own knowledge and judgement. The sailor must be encouraged to develop the ability to coach themselves, to analyse their performance objectivity, and plan the aims of their own training. They must decide their own tactics after listening to the opinions of 'experts'.

Knowledgeable parents should seek to work with the coach. If they do not agree with aspects of their teaching or sailor-handling, they should talk the matter over quietly in private.

A coach who is also a parent must not favour their own child and must ensure that their child relates to them only as a coach in the sailing environment when they are working. Otherwise the coach will lose objectivity.

International Championships

Parents are a valuable and necessary part of an international sailing team. The coach will, of course, take responsibility for training and racing matters but, as at home, the competitors will benefit from the support of one or more of their parents who can fill the following functions:

Manager / team leader: Responsible for air flights, accommodation, communication with the organisation, going to meetings, living with the team and looking after their needs such as food, laundry, health care, transport and off the water activities.

Bosun: Transporting and packing boats, checking and setting up charter boats to suit each sailor, modification of boats during measurement, on-going repairs, help afloat during training, launching and recovery assistance, security.

Helping The Coach

Most parents will, of course, come as spectators, but almost invariably their children will appreciate their presence even if they do not acknowledge it. It's always good having supporters about, and the team will be lifted by them. If there is a serious problem with a child, their parent's unique experience can also be invaluable in sorting matters out.

A parent may be asked by the coach or team leader to keep an eye on the noticeboard for changes to the sailing instructions, collection of results, notices of protests against competitors, notices of meetings, and so on. Parents can also be very useful in helping to get boats measured, being careful to minimise the effects of this stressful time on the competitors.

Parents must, however, defer to the wishes of the coach if he considers that a sailor would benefit from less parental contact. It is sometimes difficult for a parent to appreciate that, in the highly charged atmosphere of an international event, their tensions are being passed on to their child.

Parents can be a great support at international events

CHAPTER 15

The Perfect Coach

Optimist coaching is a rewarding experience, from the sheer fun of a group of kids surfing and shouting their way downwind in a force 6 to the agony and pure thrill of supporting talented competitors in an international regatta.

Coaching to national standard involves repeatedly going over theory until it is absorbed. Boat handling and basic exercises must be practised until boat control is reflex control, and confidence and ability are high. Top national sailors will mostly have the knowledge to get to top international standard. Their challenge is to use that knowledge effectively. This requires a different kind of coaching in which encouragement, facilitation, and technical support become more important, as the competitor develops his own sailing and self-coaching skills.

The step between top national and top international standard is enormous. Sailors fail to grasp the amount of work required. The coach is teacher / trainer, friend, performance analyst, motivator, disciplinarian, counsellor, facilitator, technical expert, researcher, manager / administrator and publicity agent.

Teaching
Teaching advanced racing knowledge and skills is a prime function of an Optimist coach.

Training
This involves setting up appropriate exercises afloat and ashore to aid development of top racing skills.

Planning
The racing year must be planned around major targeted events to enable the racers to reach peak performance at those times. Every year's training programme should cover all aspects of dinghy racing. With national team selection trials in April / May and major national and international championships in July / August, squads in the northern hemisphere should run through the winter, with polishing sessions before the championships.

Talks & Discussions
A young person's attention span varies from about 5 minutes at age ten to 20 minutes plus at age fifteen. Plan to break talks with questions, demonstrations, pictures or a quiz to maintain interest. Talks must be short and simple, but not childish. Complex concepts must be explained clearly and simply using drawings, model boats and demonstration. Lengthy boring topics like the racing rules can be covered in 10-minute blocks, with revision during debriefs when actual incidents are discussed. Be prepared to abort a talk and go afloat if the audience's concentration is lost.

Use 'Speak Show Do': describe something, demonstrate it, and then get them to try it. In their first year, younger sailors may not retain or fully appreciate the significance of some information but, after going over the subject for a couple of years, the same sailors become capable of giving the lectures!

Use regular recall to fix things in the mind. This can be done before starting on the main topic of the day or can be brought into the 'debrief' periods.

It is very effective when top sailors comment and contribute as much as possible. Plan talks when sailors are fresh – first thing, or after lunch. Advanced topics can be covered at the end of the day as an option for more mature competitors.

A coaching session

Communication

Do your very best to prevent any sailor losing face during training. Don't use sarcasm, make jokes or encourage laughter at the expense of young or sensitive individuals.

Don't use questions that imply that a sailor has or may have made an error. It is better to avoid starting questions with 'Why?' as this implies criticism. Try starting with 'What? When? Where? How much? How many?'. Help competitors to express how they are getting on and what they think about something, by developing an effective questioning technique.

Start with general questions and then focus down to more specific questions using simple words. If you ask a question you must listen carefully to the answer, think about it, and use their words to shape the next question. This will increase a sailor's awareness and will help them formulate new answers and ideas. Above all, keep the fun in all aspects of training and competition, with varied activities and lots of breaks for snacks.

Typical Training Day Timetable

09.00	Get changed, rigged and ready to sail
10.00	Recall of practical and theoretical points from previous day
10.05	Talk / discussion
10.25	Racing rules (one rule or incident)
10.35	Briefing and goal setting for the day
10.40	Launch
10.55	Boat handling
11.25	Starting exercises
13.00	Ashore
13.15	Debrief / video / lunch
13.30	Talk / discussion / rules
13.50	Briefing
13.55	Launch
14.10	Boatspeed work (in pairs)
14.30	Match racing
15.45	Race (long)
17.00	Ashore, change, boats away
17.20	Debrief / video / tea
17.40	Chats with individual sailors
18.00	Home

Briefing / Debriefing

Before going afloat, it is important to outline the aim of the session, and to detail the activities that will take place.

On returning ashore, each activity will be discussed, and their values assessed. Each sailor should be encouraged to say how they got on. Any incidents can be talked through, and lessons drawn. The debrief is probably the most important session of the day, for here fun afloat can be used to illustrate important points of theory in an easily understood way. At the end of any session it is vital that the sailors are able to have a chat with you privately to air a problem or to sort out an idea.

Getting To Know The Sailors

- Spend a lot of time together in training, and learn how they react afloat and ashore, body language used, and so on.
- Always be available for a chat about anything at the sailing club, at home, and on the phone.
- Get to know each sailor's parents, home situation and ability at school, in order to be aware of outside influences.
- Recognise an individual's response to the stress of competition and help each person to find ways of coping.
- Recognise how best to give support when things go wrong. Emotions can be difficult – anger, frustration or disappointment must be controlled or contained, or performance will suffer.
- Get to know a sailor's social skills – the ability to fit in a group and interact happily. Shy loners need help to establish their place in the group.

Performance Analysis

Performance analysis should be done in a number of different ways:
- By the coach: Use careful observation to identify strengths and weaknesses.
- By the sailor: Use post-race questionnaires and target charts. The coach may spot unrecognised weaknesses.
- By another sailor: Use a pair-training buddy.

Watch for competitors who set themselves unrealistic goals and are never satisfied as a result. Encourage realistic goal setting.

Building Confidence

Encourage logs or scrapbooks – with each good result confidence will grow. Some sailors, particularly girls, find starting difficult due to pushy, over-confident children. Tell them they're good, remind them of successes, do exercises in which they have to get to certain points on the line under pressure. Make sure they know the starting

rules backwards and can shout "Protest" and keep concentrating on the start all at the same time. Promote confidence in being able to sail in any weather, anytime, anywhere, so they know that there is nothing to fear from wind and water.

Giving Praise

Look for things to praise in all sailors but be selective with praise in top performers – praise effort and performance more than results.

Believe in his / her potential, but do not expect faultless, perfect and mature sailing all the time. When an error occurs, don't hold back praise for the good sailing. Remember that sailors do not mean to make errors; they will recognise them and will feel deeply disappointed with a poor result.

We have all been in the situation where we have known exactly what to do, but in the race everything went wrong. It is one of the marvellous things about sailing that conditions vary constantly, and victory is seldom certain. The place of the coach is to support rather than criticise.

As well as formal sessions, go through things in the boat park

Promoting Self-Coaching

Encourage the sailors:
- To think independently and objectively
- To analyse their own strengths and weaknesses, and to use that knowledge to establish realistic training and long term aims
- To develop on-going performance analysis skills to enable them to monitor progress towards those aims
- To identify negative emotions and cope with them in competition

Team Spirit

Optimist sailing is an individual sport but needs other sailors to help you along the way. It's very difficult to improve sailing on your own. So, even if it is an individual sport, you need to foster a team environment. This makes it more fun for everyone and the journey is more rewarding with others!
- Try logos on clothing
- Try a flag or logo on boats, sailing kit, bags, cars
- Use a team coach boat which easily recognisable
- Have a WhatsApp or Facebook group to improve communication
- Work on your personal image too

Team kit

Discipline

Practise the behaviour you expect from your sailors; be fair, considerate, and understanding. As a coach you have to be judge and executioner, and after a long day's training you may be tired and not as discerning as usual. Certain activities, the worst of which is team racing, cause emotionally charged incidents to occur between tired sailors. Summary rulings can lead to frustration and anger, whether or not the ruling was correct.

Minor transgressions are usually best overlooked. More serious cases may be called over to the coach boat. Usually a quiet, understanding but stern word will settle matters. If there is an argument between two squad members, call both over to the boat and sort matters out. Speak quietly and be totally fair and impartial. If it's clear that the sailor cannot control himself, suggest that he sits out the next exercise. The ultimate sanction would be to send someone ashore, but this is a rare last resort.

Remember that emotional outbursts may be due not just to immediate circumstances, but also to hormonal changes of puberty, shyness, parent problems, relationship problems, money worries, or school worries.

Other Coach Roles

When at a regatta, the coach has added responsibilities:
- To help the sailors understand the sailing instructions, cope with protests, deal with aggravations
- To be an information gatherer for the team on tides, weather forecasts, expert opinion, new ideas
- To provide or find the answer to any relevant questions, providing the information top sailors need to consider in their challenge for top results
- To encourage sailors to be independent decision makers on the water and responsible on the shore

Coaching Scenarios

Being a coach isn't always the same, there are different scenarios you may be working in:

- Squad coaching of a top national, area or club group of competent racing sailors over several years. Ideal group size: 8-12.
- Short term coaching of a team in preparation for a major event.
- Individual coaching of an outstanding top sailor. Most Olympic sailors are coached individually or share a coach with up to two other competitors. This is unusual in the Optimist class, although some parents try to fulfil this role.

Squad Coaching

With groups of 12 sailors or less, this is the most satisfying and productive arrangement. It is unusual for a sailor to be at the top of the Optimist class for more than four years. Long term coaching over this period will be very beneficial.

A good coach will encourage his racers to listen to other experts and collect information from every possible source. Such coaching is best done on a club or area basis. Sailors should be invited to join the training group, when they are capable of completing a club race, they want to race, they are capable of self-rescue and they have suitable equipment.

This type of group should ideally train for a period of at least six months.

Short Term Coaching

Short term coaching of a team preparing for a major event usually takes the form of 2-4 weekends and a week spent at the championship venue immediately before the event. It is likely that you will know the sailors fairly well, but the training periods should be used to get to know much more about them, their attitudes to the competition, their parents and their peers.

Work with each sailor, identifying their aims, and their perceived strengths and weaknesses. Develop personal plans for the training period and re-assess by phone or email mid-week after each training session. Build up an idea of how they react to stress, successes and failures. Develop a support plan for each sailor.

Afloat, use buddy training for tuning, speed and windshift spotting practice; sailing up opposite sides of the course to confirm wind bends and sea breeze effects. Work on starting (particularly port end), acceleration, mid-line judging and mark rounding. Match racing develops boatspeed and race winning skills. Team racing is fun and should be used for relaxation, but it can become excessively aggressive and should be tightly controlled.

Generally, make sure that whatever you organise allows individuals to cover their own training aims, and don't neglect to gather tidal and meteorological information for the area where the racing will be held well before the event.

Coaching At Competitions

Boat Measurement

This is a stressful time, even if nothing is found to be wrong.

You must be present to talk with the measurers about any perceived infringement. Check with an up-to-date copy of the class rules to make sure that the interpretation is correct, or that alternative interpretations may be as valid. An appeal to the chief measurer should always be considered if necessary.

It is good for morale to get measured as early as possible, but there is always the risk that you will get involved in that year's controversial rule interpretation. These are always sorted out before the event but can worry competitors for days. Keep cool, positive, and confident in your handling of measurement problems, and your sailors will stay calm too.

If modifications are needed to the boats or their gear, delegate this, if possible, to a competent parent. You must keep on top of other measurement questions, keeping the team occupied and supporting the anxious helm.

Boat measurement can be a stressful time

Focus On The Competition

Go over the sailing instructions with the sailors as soon as they are available, and make sure they fully understand them. Recall important and unusual points at subsequent briefings.

On the morning of the first race, keep the team focused and positive with early boat checks and rigging; plus a briefing / discussion covering tide predictions, wind, possibility of shifts, as well as the programme and arrangements for the day. The sailors must be given information clearly and accurately before going afloat.

Give your advice, but do not order your team to all "Start at the port end and sail up the left side of the course". The predictions of even top international coaches should not be trusted by sailors to the extent that they follow the plan whatever happens. A top sailor is in a better position to see what's going on in a race and should be encouraged to think for themselves and decide what to do without fear of criticism when they come ashore.

Afloat

Use the coach boat to get out to the race area an hour before racing starts if possible, towing the team if the wind is light. Check wind and tide at both the start and windward mark area if possible, and report back to the squad by which time they will have done their tuning and shift tracking runs.

Take a look at all sails and help readjust rigs or reassure the racers. Anchor and discuss tactics and ideas. Withdraw outside the race area when required by the sailing instructions, and watch the start if possible from the favoured end of the line.

The coach helping their sailors before the race

It is almost impossible to see what is going on in big fleet racing, so during the races try to relax and keep tracking wind and tide. After the race, the guys who have done well will come alongside first. Congratulate them and find out what happened, where they started, what the wind did and how their speed was.

If you have a large group, make sure the later finishers can come alongside and talk to you. They may or may not want to talk things over. You should know them well enough to know what to do. Feed them, fix anything, and offer them the chance to come aboard for a rest. In good time for the next start, get them doing warming up exercises before focusing on the next start.

Going Ashore

After the last race of the day, cruise up to each sailor in turn, and praise / encourage as merited. Give them something to eat and drink, and tow them in if the wind is light. Don't try or encourage discussion of the day's racing until later, to enable the competitors to come to terms with their results and look at their performance objectively. Ask parents to respect this rule; ideally the parents should not discuss the race with the competitor until after the debrief. The boats must be checked and packed away and the sailors changed, showered and fed.

Protests

Before heading home, the coach should wait for the end of 'Protest Time', to check for protests against the team or alterations to the sailing instructions for the next day.

Protests are daunting for a young competitor at his first international event. Help by getting the protest form and rule book, and calmly talk over the incident. Guide the sailor to the most effective form of presentation of the case, both on paper and before the committee. Just by being present during the wait for the hearing, you will be a comfort and help to your team member.

The protest committee should allow you as a coach to go in the protest as an observer. This can be very helpful in debriefing the sailor on how they did in a protest and understanding the outcome of the protest. Do check with the sailor that it is ok to observe: this can make some sailors more nervous, but encourage them since it is so beneficial.

Check for protests

Debrief

Hold the debrief for the day's racing at a pre-arranged time. Each race should be carefully analysed, and race-winning points noted. The coach should be available to speak to each competitor in turn privately. This gives the chance to go over any negative feelings. Hopefully perspectives will change, and a more positive attitude will be achieved.

Parents with experience and insight may contribute to the debrief, but you must be aware of possible inhibiting or attitude-modifying effects they will have on their offspring. This can be assessed in the pre-regatta training period; if in doubt about any parent, all should be excluded from the debrief.

Hold a debrief after racing

Coaching Equipment

The coach boat must be easily manoeuvrable with light steering and smooth throttle control. It is useful if the throttle control is on the left-hand side to make it easier to video for right handed coaches. A rigid-bottom inflatable-type boat is most suitable at sea, although cases can be made for other boat types in particular circumstances – for instance a Zodiac-type soft-bottom inflatable is seaworthy, versatile and easy to carry when deflated.

Your boat must have ground tackle that will hold in all conditions – at sea an anchor of adequate size with at least 4m of chain and plenty of warp. It should also carry a waterproof tool kit with a plug spanner, a spare set of plugs, a spare prop and cotter pins, an emergency starting rope, an emergency fuel can and a tow line.

Other equipment you need:
- **Race marks**: You will need at least two buoys, with anchors and warps. Small Dahn buoys with flags are practical.
- **Sound signal**: Cheapest and easiest is a whistle. Make sure it is loud enough. A good referee's whistle is recommended.
- **Sail battens**: Use them to signal start sequences.
- **Hand-bearing compass / flag**: Use for windshift tracking.
- **Watertight box**: Use to carry a selection of the following according to coaching circumstances: VHF hand-held radio; clipboard and paper, pens and pencils; knife, pliers, screwdriver, small adjustable spanner; plastic tape, sailpalm, needle and thread; adhesive sail repair tape and scissors; shackles, sail ties, length of light low-stretch line; rule book; sunglasses, sunscreen; wind gauge; binoculars.

- **Tide stick**: To gauge the flow of the tide (can be used in conjunction with hand-held GPS).
- **Video camera** or a waterproof phone for videoing.
- **For major events**: Spare foils, mast, sprit, ropes; food and drink for the troops; a large team or national flag.

Video Afloat

Video can be used to demonstrate good technique and tactics; as an aid to tuning; and visualisation and mental rehearsal.

However, there are some negatives which need to be borne in mind:
- It can be boring for sailors to watch lots of it – be selective
- Taking pictures from a small boat in anything but calm weather can make you feel sick and can be difficult to watch
- When used to demonstrate errors, it can lead to the competitor concerned suffering a loss of self-confidence

It is best for the coach to take their own video. They know what they want to show the sailors and what is important. Also, the coach can get very good at keeping the camera steady and they are normally driving the RIB, which is often the most stable part of the boat.

Great care needs to be taken while videoing and driving one-handed. Keep an eye on where you are going and what is happening around you, not just the video camera. With practice, this becomes easier.

When videoing, try to get close to the action, avoid using zoom

Shooting Tips

- Try to keep the horizon at the same position in the frame
- Beware of using full zoom – it will magnify the camera's movement
- Never shoot into the sun except for artistic effect
- Shooting angles should be either at right angles to the direction of movement or from ahead / astern
- Ensure you are close enough to the boat to be able to see any important points

At events it is often difficult to get close enough to get really good video, but it can often be used to show tactical and strategic situations. Consider taking pictures that can be blown up if you are too far away to video.

Replay

Know what point you are trying to make when you show the video. First time show the video without comments. Second time make comments that are positive, constructive and not pointed.

Invite sailors to comment on their own tactics. Invariably they will know what they should have done, and don't need anybody else to point it out to them! Don't show videos that don't illustrate anything of use to the sailor.

Use videos to illustrate points

Monitoring Race Progress

Both in training and in a major event it is useful to record positions at every opportunity. This helps you to keep in touch with each individual's progress. It is easy to watch those that are doing well but lose touch with what is happening to the others. Later you will find it very handy to be able to show a disappointed sailor that they did at least do a brilliant second beat. A good method is to record windward mark placings for various promising sailors is like this:

Sailor	1st Wdwd	2nd Wdwd	3rd Wdwd	Finish
Becky	10	12	11	12
Jim	40	30	36	37

Target Chart

A target chart is useful as a means of evaluating a sailor's perceived ability and self-confidence. It is handy as a starting point for discussing training aims. Each sector concerns a particular skill. Sailors assess their ability in that skill on a score of 1-10 and shade in the sector accordingly.

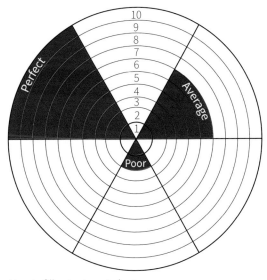

How to fill out a target chart

TARGET CHART

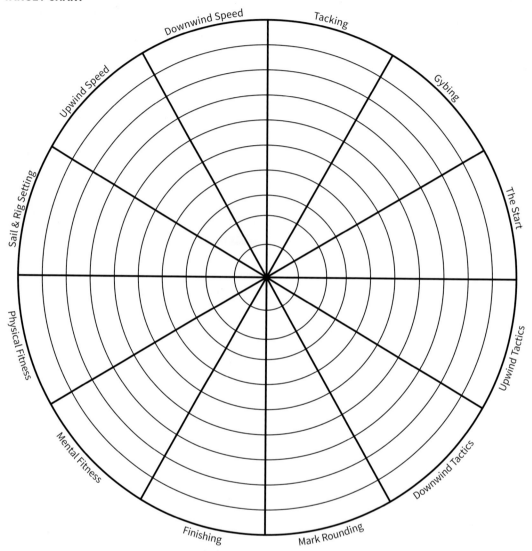

You can rate yourself on this target chart on the topics we have covered in this book.

You can also use Training Record Sheets and Race Training Analysis Sheets (see next two pages).

These all can be downloaded from www.fernhurstbooks.com. Search for *Optimist Racing* and then click on 'Additional Resources'.

OPTIMIST TRAINING RECORD SHEET

Team			Date	
Venue	Wind direction		Wind Strength	Sea state

Sail	Mast Rake	Luff Tension	Outhaul

Session & goals

Hours sailed:

Venue notes

Speed notes

What did you do & learn

Review - what do you need to do next

RACE TRAINING ANALYSIS SHEET

Report No:	Event:	Date:
Helm:	Sail No:	Boat Name:
Sail make:	Sail Cut:	Sail Age:

Wind Strength (steady? shifty? gusty?):

Sea State (smooth? choppy? swell?):

Waves (direction? effects? technique used?):

Luff Tension (number of twists on tack diagonal tie):

Luff Shape (convex? straight? concave?):

Top Tie Gap:	Tack Tie Gap:	Luff Tie Gap:

Outhaul Tension / Foot Shape:

Mast Rake:

Daggerboard (vertical? forward? back? raised? how many cm?):

Beat trim (upright? heeled to leeward? heeled to windward?):

Balance (weather? lee? neutral helm?):

Speed Upwind:

Speed Downwind:

Specific Problems:

Answers / Comments:

RACING NOTES

Pre-start:	Start:
1st beat:	Weather mark:
Good points:	Problems:
Finish:	Comments:

WIND STRATEGY

David Houghton & Fiona Campbell

ROXANNE

SAIL TO WIN

CHAPTER 5

Wind Facts: Gusts & Lulls

The wind varies on every timescale, from seconds to minutes to hours to days and even longer. It is the short period variations in the order of minutes which are normally described as gusts and lulls.

Gusts & Lulls Due To Thermal Overturning

We saw in Chapter 2 that many gusts and lulls are a result of air overturning near the sea or land surface when the air aloft, which has not been slowed or backed by friction at the surface, comes down to replace what has been subject to friction. A common cause of this overturning is thermal; when air warmed at the surface becomes buoyant, rises, and is replaced by air from aloft. This is the most easy to understand.

On many days, particularly when there is a regular pattern of cumulus clouds, the gusts and lulls arrive at fairly regular intervals. In these conditions the normal surface wind is blowing in the normal way and super-imposed on it is an overturning motion, upwards underneath the cumulus clouds and downwards between them (below). The descending air has not experienced friction near the surface so it has approximately the horizontal speed and direction of the gradient wind. It is significantly veered and stronger than the wind which has spent some time near the surface. In other words it is a gust. The air under each cloud has spent time near the surface, has been slowed and backed by friction – it is a lull. Thermally driven gusts and lulls have one clearly defined characteristic: a gust is always veered and stronger in contrast with a lull, which is always backed and lighter.

Timescale & Size Of Shift

If the cumulus clouds are small and relatively close together they indicate a relatively short time between gusts and lulls – perhaps 3 minutes or so. The swing in wind is typically in the order of 5 to 10 degrees in direction and 5 to 10 per cent in speed. If the clouds are larger and further apart the time interval is indicated – perhaps 10 to 15 minutes – and the shifts may be less regular and larger. If the convection becomes so deep that the cumulus clouds turn into cumulonimbus and showers develop, completely different wind characteristics are experienced. They are described in Chapter 15.

Gust   Lull

(Stronger veered   (Air has slowed
wind from aloft)   & backed)

The clouds causing gusts & lulls

Gradient Wind Blowing Along Line Of Valley

The surface wind will blow approximately in the same direction as the gradient, but its strength will depend on the stability of the air in the valley, and whether the valley is closed or open. If the valley provides a clear route through a mountain range the wind will funnel strongly along it, particularly when the air is stable and therefore reluctant to rise over the mountains (below).

Open valley funnelling the wind

Gradient Wind Blowing Across Valley

The air flow is likely to separate, and the steeper the slope the more readily it separates. The eddy forms on the side of the valley towards the gradient wind. The steeper the side the larger the eddy (A is larger than B in the diagram below).

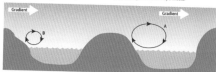

Gradient wind blowing across the valley creates an eddy – the steeper the slope, the longer the eddy

Peninsulas

Let's look first at a relatively small peninsula, the size of Cornwall or Auckland, for instance. In the absence of a gradient wind, on a sunny day a sea breeze develops onto all shores (below), but the breezes onto the opposite major shores dominate and progress inland until they meet in the middle of the peninsula where a line of cumulus clouds may be seen. Once the two breezes meet they die. Then after 10 to 20 minutes or so the land warms again and the sea breeze process starts all over. To sustain sea breezes onto both shores throughout the afternoon without faltering the peninsula must be in the order of 100 km wide.

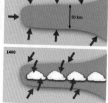

Sea breeze cycle on a 50 km peninsular

Spain

Spain is a good example of a very large peninsula, and winds around Spain in the summer are a good example of a Quadrant 3 situation. For much of the summer the weather map shows a shallow low pressure area over the country, and each day the pressure falls some 3 to 5 millibars due to the heating of the land, recovering at night. The detailed shape of the isobars varies from day to day. It is often influenced by thunderstorms breaking out in late afternoon and continuing into the night, especially in late summer. On average the morning gradient wind is parallel to the coast and just in Quadrant 3, light southerly on the Mediterranean coast, light northerly on the Atlantic coast, and so on. Every afternoon the thermal vector, also

In the diagram top right, the direction of the gradient wind is along the line of the peninsula. The most significant feature is the bands of stronger and lighter winds respectively to be found just offshore. It is important to note that it will take only a small swing in wind direction to support a sea breeze onto one of the major shores. Starting from a wind parallel to the axis of the peninsula, a shift of only 5 degrees may tip the balance in favour of a sea breeze onto one or other shore, a shift probably outside the accuracy of the forecast. The onus is on you, the sailor on the spot, to interpret the wind trends observed on the water.

The middle diagram is a case for a good Quadrant 1 sea breeze onto the downwind shore, but a peninsula width of over 70 km is probably necessary for its full strength potential to be reached. Sea breezes generally penetrate inland at a speed of between 10 and 20 km per hour. From your knowledge of the width of the peninsula you can make a very rough estimate of how long it will be before it gets to the other shore and starts to die.

The peninsula situation in the bottom diagram is interesting. The breeze starts onto the end at B, a Quadrant 1 situation, but as it veers and bends to the coastline it increases on the more southerly-facing coast, and dies away at B with some bending of the wind around the corner.

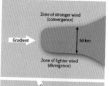

Zone of stronger wind
(convergence)

Gradient

50 km

Zone of lighter wind
(divergence)

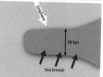

Gradient

70 km

Sea breeze

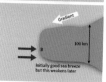

Gradient

100 km

B

Initially good sea breeze
but this weakens later

The effect of the gradient wind on different sized peninsulas

parallel to the coast, enhances the morning wind to give an afternoon onshore wind typically in the range of Force 2 to 4 at an angle of about 15 to 20 degrees to the coast. It is blowing onshore but is not a sea breeze, and does not have the important characteristic of a sea breeze, which is to be strongest close to the coast.

TRAINING TO WIN

Jon Emmett

SAIL TO WIN

Stepping Stone Upwind

Sail to the windward mark, and round correctly, sail downwind for 2 boat lengths with sail controls etc. fully adjusted for the downwind and then stop. Then use a Rabbit Start to start again upwind to a new windward mark which you round, sail downwind for 2 boat lengths and then stop. And then repeat with another Rabbit Start and upwind leg to a new windward mark, and so on.

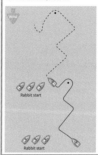

Rabbit start

Rabbit start

This exercise could also be used as a way of progressing to the intended race area rather than towing, or an extended warm-up for getting to a race area, or a way of taking people back to shore and keeping them focused.

Depending upon the venue, it may be extremely important to train on the precise race area to experience the same currents, waves, wind, etc.

Keelboat-Style Steering

Going fast in any boat is about steering the optimum angle to the next mark and so this is a good exercise to focus on steering, separate from the other elements of hiking / trapezing and trimming we discussed earlier. It is all too easy to steer too much or just use all your bodyweight to 'bully' the boat around the course, especially if you are young and fit. So, in this exercise, you sit 'keelboat-style': sitting on the side deck but in reverse, with your legs pointing out (be careful not to drag your feet in the water as it will slow you down). This means that your body weight is fixed and it may even be hard to sheet. This makes good steering suddenly the main focus of your attention.

Sailing keelboat style

This exercise can be easy or difficult:

Easy	Free sailing keelboat style
Medium	Sail around a course keelboat style
Hard	Racing keelboat style

Advanced Techniques

Holding A Lane

Very often after a start you must hold your lane (continuing on your existing tack at good VMG without being affected by the boats around you through dirty air / leebow effect etc.) because otherwise you will get bad air or have to sail a lot of extra distance:

- If you try to go low, then you may end up being leebowed by the boat to leeward
- If you try to pinch, someone to windward is likely to roll you and give you dirty air as well
- If you tack you may have to duck many boats and sail a greater distance

In these scenarios it is best to keep going (as fast as you can!) until an opportunity presents itself to do something different.

So, being able to hold your lane is very important. The higher the level of competition the more important this becomes.

Often you may have to hold your lane with other boats in very close proximity, either because you definitely want to go one way (for example, if there is an expected shift or there is better current) or because you are not in a position to tack without having to duck a lot of boats and thereby lose a lot of places.

Lane Hold

Wind

Start line

The perfect exercise for this is the Lane Hold: there is a standard 3,2,1, go sequence, but the aim is to get upwind on one tack to level with a buoy, perhaps a 3-minute sail upwind.

Of course, in a real race, after a poor start a boat may be able to get out of the dirty air / leebow effect by footing off (losing some ground to windward but better than sailing in dirty air) or tacking off (again getting into clear air). But the point of this exercise is to learn when you can hold a clear lane and when you can't. The narrower the lane you can hold the better, so pushing it to the limit in training will help you understand this.

After the start, try to hold your lane for 3 minutes

Rabbit Start

It is not always possible to have starting marks or, indeed, someone to monitor the line. A Rabbit Start is a great way of starting an exercise and it also practises your ability to judge speed and distance.

Rabbit Start

The 'Rabbit' sails across the fleet on a close-hauled course (very important they don't reach in at speed as everyone has to be able to judge their approach). Boats then cross at full speed, on a close-hauled course behind the Rabbit.

When everyone has passed behind the Rabbit, the Rabbit tacks (maybe 2 boats past the last boat, but this is wind strength and boat class dependent).

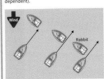

Wind

Rabbit

Rabbit Start

Controlling The Boat

The most important thing is controlling the boat. The advanced exercises overleaf will really push some of you to practise on your own, others in groups. These are time and distance / boat handling exercises. Remember that, even though you will typically be lining up on starboard tack on a start line, you should also practise on port tack because these are incredibly useful boat handling exercises in their own right.

There are individual exercises and group exercises shown overleaf.

THE
ANDREW
SIMPSON
SAILING FOUNDATION

The charity was founded to honour the life and legacy of Andrew 'Bart' Simpson MBE, Olympic Gold & Silver medalist and America's Cup Sailor by using sailing to improve the lives of young people.

Working with sailing providers internationally, the Foundation offers the challenges of a sailing environment to promote health and wellbeing, and to develop personal skills that will improve a young person's ability to succeed in life.